Navigating
Indieworld

A Beginner's Guide to
Self-Publishing
And Marketing Your Book

Julie A. Gerber
and Carole P. Roman

First Printing: August 2016
ISBN-13: 978-1537228068
ISBN-10: 1537228064

To my sons, Michael and Eric, who got the ball rolling, my husband, David, for keeping it moving, and Julie Gerber, who caught it! ~ Carole

To my family for always encouraging me to follow my dreams. To Carole, for pushing me to expand those dreams. Your friendship means the world to me. ~ Julie

For Sarah Noffke, thank you for sharing your lovely world with us.

Special thanks to Sharon Isbell and Keith Katsikas for their valuable feedback.

Warm gratitude to artist Kelsea Wierenga for all her helpful tips on illustrators and Conny Crisalli for her gentle patience as she corrected our editing mistakes.

Disclosure

Although the authors and publisher have made every effort to ensure that the information in this book was correct at press time, the authors and publisher do not assume and hereby disclaim any liability to any party for any loss, damage, or disruption caused by errors or omissions, whether such errors or omissions result from negligence, accident, or any other cause.

This book should serve only as a general guide and not as the ultimate source of subject information. Within this book, you will find a list of services that many authors purchase. We feel that it is necessary to include them along with the estimated prices (which are subject to change) you can expect to pay if you make the decision to hire someone for these services. We also made every effort to list alternatives as well as resources to help you curb the cost of self-publishing and marketing your book. This book contains information that might be dated and is intended only to educate and entertain. The authors and publisher shall have no liability or responsibility to any person or entity regarding any loss or damage incurred or alleged to have incurred, directly or indirectly, by the information contained in this book. You hereby agree to be bound by this disclaimer, or you may return this book within the guarantee period for a full refund.

In the interest of full disclosure, this book contains the names of companies and people we have worked with and some we haven't. Neither Julie A. Gerber or Carole P. Roman are receiving any form of monetary compensation, physical products, services, discounts, or favors from the companies or authors as payment for being featured or mentioned in this book. We are not using affiliate links. The companies, authors, or blogs mentioned have not endorsed the authors or this book. This is our way of paying it forward, helping those who have helped us by sharing information and their experiences, and yes, we may even draw a little attention to a few companies that we are connected to through our books or our everyday lives. Do your part and research everyone you consider working with, read reviews online, and ask others before using any company mentioned in this book. The authors made the decision to self-publish even though Julie is affiliated with a publishing company because this book is about self-publishing. While the authors and publisher take no responsibility for the business practices of these companies or the performance of any product or service, the authors or publisher have used many of the products or services and make a recommendation in good faith based on their experiences. These are provided for informational purposes only and do not constitute an endorsement of any products or services provided by these websites and that the links are subject to change, expire, or be redirected without any notice.

Follow us on Facebook for more tips! Facebook.com/NavigatingIndieworld

TABLE OF CONTENTS

INTRODUCTION

A funny thing happened on the way to my retirement. I found myself entering a whole new career in my late fifties, joining a community of people from which there was no return. I entered Indieworld.

A different breed of people live there, yet we all have the same agenda. It's an amazing place - we don't see our differences. We are color, age, and gender blind. We only want to tell our story and have it be appreciated. Oh yes, and make a small fortune in the process.

Indieworld is a vast entity filled with a universe of people driven to do the same thing. They are seeking what I refer to as the three "Fs": fame, fortune, and fulfillment without getting screwed. I bet you thought I was going to use another word.

It's been four years since I fell through the rabbit hole of independent publishing, and I feel the motivation to give back to my people. This is for the endless population of folks who are loitering on social media, crammed on Goodreads, and filling up blogs, who are lost and don't know how to get on the track to succeed.

If any chapter of this book makes it easier for one of our brethren and they make it to *Fifty Shades of Gray* status, then we feel we have done our job. A best-seller for one of us is a victory for all of Indiekind.

This is making me feel like an independent author superhero, and every one of those has a valiant sidekick. A brave individual ready to take on the dark forces of bad reviews, expensive publicity, and the black hole of a four-digit high-rating number on Amazon.

The partner in my quest for the three "Fs" is Julie Gerber, the head guru at Away We Go Media. She is the wonder woman of social media, the empress of Twitter, the princess of Pinterest, and a maverick riding the ups and downs of Facebook. She has become a vital part of our process and a member of our family. I could not have done it without her.

We will approach the subject to educate, prepare, and enable any person to write, publish, and ultimately sell their books to the general public. This is our story.

Carole P. Roman
Long Island, New York

CHAPTER 1

GENESIS ~ CAROLE

Let's start with Genesis, the beginning, the tiny seed of an idea that roots itself in your brain crying out to be nurtured.

It ignites with a spark, the light that illuminates the recesses of your mind, making the wheels start to whirl feverously.

The thoughts refuse to be extinguished. They needle, interrupting your daily chores, making you stare off into space and think. You shelve it; you have too much to do, but it percolates, the "what ifs" bubbling up until they erupt in a cataclysmic explosion that finally forces you to take your computer in hand and gaze at the white screen that turns your face red with the heat of embarrassment. Can you do this?

Writing a book is subjective. It's a highly personal experience. You are taking your deepest thoughts, your fears, perceptions and laying them out like a smorgasbord for the world to read, peruse, and finally, judge you based on their personal point of view. Sometimes they are brutal, flaying the words from your book like a marauder. Other times, you will strike a communal chord, touching their heart and soul in the most intimate way. Either way, it is one of the most rewarding experiences in the world.

Your subject or story means everything to you. You can plot and plan, but somehow they take on a life of their own. Don't obsess about what you are writing. You may find that like the childhood game of telephone, your book has morphed somehow and is a completely different story from where you began. In the end, it won't matter; keep the momentum going, and let it develop organically. Once your characters take the lead, it becomes their story and not yours. Push to the finish line. As soon as you complete it, you'll find out that is when the hard work really starts. Jump into the world of indie writers.

You will find plenty of experts to help you take your project from idea to a finished work of art. Amazon and the internet are filled with books to help you through the nuts and bolts of writing a book.

I got started writing when most people are thinking about jettisoning work and lightening their load. My sons dared me to take on the challenge. After all, I had talked about it my entire life. It was a long time dream, put on the back burner, the demands of family and business eclipsing my passion.

I didn't know where to begin. My son urged me to sit and start writing. You don't need special tools or carved out time. It could be while you're waiting for the kids at practice, when you are on the train, or in my case, at my desk, in the office, before everyone arrived to begin the workday.

Experts say, write about what you know. I don't agree with that. Write about what you want to know. Write about what you love or hate. Write about what you want. If we all wrote about what we know, do you think there would be so many choices on Amazon in science fiction or fantasy?

All that matters is you enjoy it and finish it. You could be the one to make a fortune and become the next literary breakout. Maybe you won't. Either way, you are leaving a permanent marker that you were here. You are sending out a piece of yourself to our vast universe to mingle with other notions. Perhaps you are going to change the world. Uh oh, did I make you feel self-conscious?

Don't be intimidated by the thoughts rushing through your head! Once you start, your imagination will take on a life of its own.

You can't do it, you tell yourself. You feel stupid. It's silly, a childish daydream, you are thinking, but still your fingers type. You are so lost in research; nobody can have a coherent conversation with you. You're discovering things you've never known before.

Your spouse is annoyed; the kids are hungry; the boss is mad; you missed a deadline for work. It doesn't matter. All that counts are the words flowing from your speeding fingers, your shoulders shaking with mirth at your humor. It will start to take shape; the paragraphs will add up, and a story will emerge. Enjoy the sting behind your eyes at the sad turn of events for Brad, Thad, Emily, or Justin. The thrill of a chase or the crazy quilt of twists you are creating.

Check the word count. Fifteen hundred words. Is that dawn peeking under the shades? Sixty-five hundred by the following weekend. You hit twenty thousand yesterday. Did you share your creation with anyone? Did you tell your bus driver you are writing a book?

You do sleep; you still eat; you continue to perform your day job. Mindless activities like laundry are a welcome relief as you plot and plan, playing out scenarios in your mind. You function in a *Twilight Zone* of want. You want to complete the next chapter; you want to tie the threads together; you want to - finish? The computer waits on the table, mocking you, daring you to continue.

Reread or not to reread - you can. Don't let it stop you. Don't overthink it, yet they'll be others who will do that for you. Today you're like a dynamo. Just finish the darn thing!

The story is taking shape; your characters have a personality - you love them; no, maybe you hate them. They are as real to you as the faces you are cleaning up after dinner and the soft cheeks you kiss goodnight. You return to your computer with ice-cream or popcorn, whatever your comfort food of choice and continue.

So it begins, your opus, your work of art. The shaping and molding of words to echo your thoughts, your deepest, love/fear, hate/joy - it doesn't matter. It's yours, and it's here. You read it multiple times, but you need to have another opinion. It could be your spouse, lover, or friend, but the time has come to share your creation with someone who promises to be honest. It's time to launch this baby into orbit.

To Do List:

1 - Write your book.

CHAPTER 2

Is Honesty the Best Policy? Only Your Beta Reader Knows for Sure ~ Julie

Your book is complete, or is it? Maybe you missed something. Could you have taken a different turn with your characters or plot? There are thousands of ways it might have gone and didn't. Your confidence is wavering, and you are suddenly overcome with fear and doubt. You liked the story, but will readers embrace your characters and remember them after the story ends?

This world you created for yourself and others, is it believable? Did you tie up all the loose ends; are there gaffs? Did your hero start out in a suit and tie and end up in jeans without ever changing his clothes? Did the main character have blue eyes that mysteriously became brown through no fault of her own? Are there holes in your story? Or did it seem like it was written by a five-year-old? You need another opinion, someone to look for oversights in your story and help you fill in the inevitable gaps. You should have a beta reader.

What is a beta reader, and why do you need one? Maybe you don't *think* you need one but trust me, you do. Most writers rely heavily on family and friends to read and critique their works while they not so patiently await their judgment. They gush over your new book and tell you how proud they are, all while giving you a big thumbs up. They say impressive things about your wonderful writing abilities and get your hopes up about becoming the next best-seller. They aren't biased; they couldn't be. Why would family and friends tell you that your book is good enough and allow you to fall flat on your face?

I'll answer that for you. The most likely reason is they have known this was a dream of yours, and they can't stand the thought of crushing those ambitions. Can you blame them? The road to hell is paved with good intentions. I'll let you in on a little secret. The first stop on that road is an indie writer's book purgatory where the only saving grace is to pull your book, change the cover and title, and have a proper edit or rewrite. Your book will need a new identity. It will need to be reborn. Your book would have a difficult time recovering from the onslaught of negative reviews thanks to well-meaning family and friends. I've seen this happen to a few authors, and once they pulled the book and started over with unbiased help, they do well.

The best advice I can give is to get someone to read your book (before it is published) who is willing to be brutally honest. It can be hard to open yourself up to being judged, but it's a necessary part of this process and requires that we lock our egos in the closet. You need a critic that isn't afraid to ask what you were thinking and tell you that chapter you were up all night writing needs a complete rewrite.

If you have friends and family that won't hesitate to be critical in their assessment, leave you in tears with their frankness, or tell you your book sucks, and you need to start over, ask them for help. Then take them to dinner. Those are the friends you should keep.

According to Wikipedia, "a beta reader is a non-professional reader who reads a written work, generally fiction, with the intent of looking over the material to find and improve elements such as grammar and spelling, as well as suggestions to improve the story, its characters, or its setting. Beta reading is typically done before the story is released for public consumption."

You can find beta readers everywhere. They frequent authors' groups on Goodreads and Facebook. Some bloggers list it as one of their services. Many charge a fee. The rate varies from reader to reader. You can expect to pay between twenty-five and fifty dollars for every twenty thousand words or pay an hourly rate. Do your research. Ask for references, interview, and look at examples of their work. If they are good, you'll be able to see it when you pull up the book they critiqued on Amazon and note the sales ranking or awards. Read the book's online reviews to determine if the book flowed, had consistent character and plot development, and left an impression on readers. If they did a good job, the reviews would reflect it.

If you want help outside your circle of friends and family, look for beta readers that have worked with more than one author. Sometimes beta readers get lucky, and the author has all the talent. If you find one that has multiple books in their portfolio from more than one author, you will have a more accurate appraisal of their work. Talk to the authors they worked with and find out how much the beta reader helped and if they were compatible with your writing style. The last thing you need is to get attached to someone who doesn't have the passion or the drive that you do.

Being a beta reader is one of the things that I love most about my job. I love seeing that idea take root and flourish. I enjoy watching the author create these characters and plots while witnessing those elements come together in a memorable book.

Michael Phillip Cash was the first author I worked with that sent me a draft, allowing and encouraging me to scrutinize every word. I started out reading and critiquing his first books, then it evolved, and I began reading along as he wrote, thanks to the wonders of Google Drive.

Some of you may be wondering, what is Google Drive? If you remember the old Google Documents, Drive is the latest version where you can store files, sync them with others, and share files. You can allow a person to read a file, edit, or comment. Sending a file is as easy as typing in their email address. Or you can send them a unique URL (link) that will enable them to go directly to the document page. One of the best features is that you can see all the changes made to a file if you give permission for someone to make changes to the document. There will be a date, time, and list of all changes made by each person with the authorization to edit.

With Google Drive, it's easy to share ideas and thoughts and tell the author if the flow was off, or if the book was too predictable. Two sets of eyes are better than one. Many authors are so caught up in their story that they may miss the little things. The devil is in the details, and a good beta reader will keep you on track and keep your story consistent.

Not all authors write books using Google Drive, but if you are working with a beta reader, you may want to consider trying it sometime. The service makes it easy to chat on the document page while the other person is online, and that is a helpful feature if you are bringing in others to inspect and critique your work.

The bottom line is that a good beta reader will have your back and will be there either for the entire process or wait until you are confident enough to share your work. They will tell you if a character's name is throwing everything off or if your characters aren't believable enough. Use them wisely, but don't get derailed by having too many beta readers inspect your book. It's great to have a few well-read individuals read and give their opinions. However, one good beta reader is all you need. Consider the changes recommended by your beta reader. You don't have to make them all, but you should consider why the changes were suggested. Keep an open mind and make your book better than it was previously!

To Do List:

1 - Find a reliable beta reader.
2 - Patiently await feedback from your beta reader.
**3 - Consider the beta reader's suggestions and adjust if you think it
     is of the book's best interest. Don't let your ego get in the way.**

CHAPTER 3
ARE WE THERE YET? ~ JULIE

Now is the time to choose not one but at least two to three professional editors if you want to avoid debuting your novel with mistakes. If you need to stay on a budget, one will do; make sure you find someone well versed in the rules. Any editor worth their salt should have a copy of *The Chicago Manual of Style* on their desk. If they have a copy they use, you are in good hands. It doesn't count if it is used as a desk ornament. This book is the standard, and it is one of the most trusted sources for guidance on editing.

The price of editing depends on the type of editing you need. Basic copy editing can vary from one to four dollars per page and content editing, which is more extensive, runs over seven dollars a page if you are working with a freelance editor. For a full-length novel, you can pay thousands of dollars for editing. Shop around and ask for recommendations in author groups on Amazon. We used Conny Crisalli for this book.

If you are editing your book, fair warning. Any mistakes are going to be blasted in your reviews, and readers won't be gentle about it. They can be as ruthless as vultures, and they will tear apart the book that you spent so much time writing and possibly your entire life dreaming of being a good writer. Poor editing has given indie writers a bad reputation, and that is the sole reason that some readers have given up reading indie books altogether. Too much-flawed or non-existent editing spoiled it for them. If you are putting money into your book, make sure to save some for the editor. They deserve it. They are like a book stylist and make you look put together.

There are different types of editing that you can request. A soft edit is looking over the book for grammar and punctuation issues and correcting them. A hard edit is more extensive and takes longer to complete. The editor changes the text to make things flow better, rewriting some lines or paragraphs. They point out inaccuracies and let you know if something isn't clear. Don't get defensive; a good editor can make or break a book.

When you hire an editor, you can discuss what you are looking for before agreeing on a price. Editing is an important but necessary job. Find someone you can trust. Your book and reputation depend on it.

If you insist on editing the book yourself, try something old school. Take the time to print each page. Read aloud. Grab a red pen, take each page, and study each line by line. When you're done, mix up the pages, so they are out of order, and do it again or read the paragraphs or sentences in backward order. I had a friend that would check each line before and after the line she was editing. It cut out any distractions, and she was more accurate.

I've tried editing my work and found it impossible. I was too close to the content. By the time I arrived at the editing stage, I had read, written, and rewritten so many times that my brain often saw things differently than how they appeared on paper. I read the words, how I wanted them to appear instead of how they emerged from the pages of the book. The brain is an amazing thing and plays the funniest tricks; only the joke's on you if you don't catch the errors.

Grammarly is a program that you can download on your computer. There is a free version as well as a paid version that gives you a few extra perks. Download it, and it will catch many of your mistakes. It's a useful tool to have in your arsenal, but it doesn't replace an editor. If you buy the program, it runs under one hundred dollars per year.

Also understand that with the best editors, they are human and mistakes can be missed. If an editing mistake is pointed out in a review, feel free to reply that you fixed the mistake (if you made the correction) and thank the reviewer for pointing it out. Corrections are possible after it's published if the book is an e-book, print on demand, or POD publisher. Simply download the manuscript with errors, correct the mistakes, and upload again. Once it's been accepted, it will reflect the changes.

On that note, the only other times you should consider responding to a review online is to discuss a topic politely that the reader brings up and wants to know more about or to answer a question. Goodreads' policy is for an author not to engage at all, ever.

Never respond to negative comments or reviews on any of the sites. We will discuss more on that topic later.

Nevertheless, an editor is one of the best investments you can make in your journey to self-publishing. A professionally edited book gives you peace of mind and will set you up for success. You are off to a fantastic start!

To Do List:

1 - Edit your book or hire an editor or two depending on your budget.

CHAPTER 4

FORMATTING - THIS IS NOT THE PLACE TO PRACTICE ~ JULIE AND CAROLE

According to Dictionary.com, formatting is "the general physical appearance of a book, magazine, or newspaper, such as the typeface, binding, quality of paper, margins, etc."

Many readers will close a book if they are annoyed with issues in the layout or how the pages appear once printed. It can be frustrating to format a book, so this might be a place to find someone and pay them to do it for you if you have little patience for the technical details of publishing. We always pay Createspace.com for the novels and an artist for our children's books. You will have to have Kindle and e-books formatted as well.

Formatting is crucial when you load your book onto a self-publishing site. If it is done incorrectly, your book won't print properly or read well in an e-book format.

Also, when having your book published as a paperback, pay attention to which book dimensions are acceptable in both public libraries and bookstores. These venues are strict with the sizes. They must be made to fit specific shelves, and your book will not be available to mass distribution if you make that error. You can find that information by calling or writing your publishing consultant. You can also visit Createspace, click the "Books" tab at the top of the page, and look at printing options to comply with industry standards for books in both ƙe. You will also need to know those dimensions over.

ƙperience with Createspace. They suggest you ℎlable to as many sources as possible, and you ship ᵢ on the big, blue arrows indicating where you want your books ƙ. y trial and error, I learned that one of my books would not be sold at libraries because I had sized it wrong. I ended up resizing the book after I found out which dimensions were acceptable. I couldn't find the information anywhere on the site at the time, so here's where a publishing consultant would have come in handy. You have to say you want your book to have the opportunity to sell everywhere and learn the guidelines.

E-books and Kindles should be professionally formatted as well. Word-2-Kindle.com is a company that formats e-books and paperbacks, and they offer a quick turnaround with free unlimited revisions for two weeks at the time of this printing. Afterward, the charge is minimal. Kindle formatting starts at forty-nine dollars and paperbacks can be as much as two hundred dollars. Adding images or graphs will cost extra. Sometimes they may give you a better price if you are getting your paperback and e-book formatted at the same time. It's a good deal, and they are one of the most affordable companies; be sure to proof the final formatted copy to check for any errors before you upload your book to publish. If you find errors, don't try to fix them yourself. Send it back to the company that did the formatting to correct any mistakes.

There are others that will also format for a reasonable fee. There is nothing that will irritate readers and reviewers more than poorly edited or formatted books, which brings us to the next stage. A PDF, Word, Doc, Docx, or RTF file is needed to upload to Createspace. Doc/Docx or HTML format is the preferred Kindle format if you want to upload your book to Amazon, but they also accept PDF files. Those are the files to send for formatting, and once they complete the job, you will get the appropriate file back to upload and publish. Because you have a PDF or Doc file doesn't mean you get to skip formatting.

Since we are talking about files, it is smart to have a Mobi (Mobipocke or ePub (short for ePublication) file on hand for book reviewers that prefer downloaded files to Kindle gifts or paperbacks. A Kindle gift is where you buy a digital copy of your book on Amazon, and you click "send a gift." You only need the reviewer's email address, and you can include a note, thanking them for reviewing your book. The cost of sending out paperback and Kindle books can add up, so offer the Mobi or ePub versions as well when you ask for reviews. Mobi makes it easier to read for people with e-books or small screens. Also, you may need ePub files to upload or submit your book to some sites, so go ahead and have that file on hand as well.

Do you have a headache yet? Don't worry. If you have a book professionally formatted, a reputable company will send you the files you need. There are also some free conversion sites online that will convert files for you. All you do is upload your file and decide on your conversion. It takes a few minutes of your time. Julie uses Zamzar.com. They will send the converted files to your inbox. Always look over the file first before you send one out to a reviewer.

Formatting is where you will pick things like the size and type of font. Choose something that will be comfortable for the reader to read. There are all different types of fonts to use. Minion, Clarendon Serif, Garamond, Gothic, you get the picture. There are tons of them; you probably never thought about the print in anything you've read. The differences are subtle, but they have an enormous impact on your book. It seems certain fonts are genre friendly, so Google your genre and see what kinds of fonts are popular for your type of book.

If you make the decision to format your book, you should know that there are step-by-step tutorials and video classes on the web. Many of those are a direct result of the lack of information previously available online. Some authors have taken it upon themselves to share what they know. D.L. Morrese is one of them. Hugh C. Howey and his blog, theWayFinder.com, is another. I haven't formatted my books following their tutorials, but their information seems spot on and complete. They walk you through each process and show you with photos or video each

understand. It's easier if you begin in a Microsoft Word
are using Google Drive, you can download the file as a
e to get started.

To upload your book to KDP (Kindle), check out the author, Dr. Sandra
N. Peoples on YouTube.com. She gives step-by-step video instructions
that are easy to follow.

Once you have formatted your book and it is uploaded to KDP, you
can preview the book before you publish. This gives you the benefit
of seeing how the book will appear to readers on their Kindle devices,
phones, and tablets.

Formatting isn't as complicated as it seems. Does that mean I want to
do it? No, but I am eternally grateful to the authors for their thorough
explanations to guide us all through the process of formatting. If you
want to save some money, they make it easy!

To Do List:
1 - Determine the size of your book.
2 - Format your book as well as your e-book.
3 - Choose the font and page color for the inside of your book.
**4 - If you are formatting it yourself, make sure you know what you
    are doing.**

CHAPTER 5

Go Fishing ~ Julie and Carole

Now that you have a completed, edited, and professionally formatted manuscript, what are you going to do with it? Whatever you do, don't put it on a shelf and look at it a few years before you convince yourself to take the next step.

There are options. Think about your budget and consider your book. Do you want to maintain the freedom of making choices? Do you want to hand over the reins and see what happens? This is where things can get complicated.

There are at least five ways to get a manuscript published.

1 - Get into one of the big five (highly impossible unless you have an agent, but that's another story).
2 - Find one that will publish for a fee.
3 - Find one that will publish without a fee.
4 - Self-publish with a POD, using one of the many sites available on the internet.
5 - Self-publish an e-book.

1 - Big House Publishing - The Fantastic Five

If you are interested in publishing with one of the larger publishing houses, you will need a literary agent. There are many things to consider when searching for an agent. The agent's job is to pitch (sell) your book to the publishing house. The big five publishing houses happen to be Penguin Random House, Macmillan, HarperCollins, Hachette, and Simon & Schuster and can only be approached through an agent. They are also the names behind many of the smaller publishing houses. Almost all of them require a literary agent to submit your book.

Your book's value (how much money it can potentially make) will play a significant role in your ability to find an agent. Having a book in a genre or category (romance, mystery, suspense, etc.) that sells more easily will be taken into consideration. *The Writer's Market* is a helpful book that contains a listing of agents.

An agent will not get paid until they sell your book, so they are careful to make smart decisions when it comes to the authors they accept. Make sure your book is polished and edited before sending it to an agent for consideration. There is stiff competition, and you want your book to shine. Be prepared to get a lot of letters of rejection. Sometimes they won't bother to notify you. There is that wonderful chance that someone does recognize your efforts, and it will pay off. If you fail, don't be afraid to try again. Also, don't forget there are other options for success.

You need to know that a traditional publisher will assume all costs, and you will get paid royalties for sales. While the idea of someone else shouldering all of the cost to publish and promote a book can be exciting, it can be difficult to give up creative control. And you can stop reading now since you won't need any of the following information. Those book companies have armies of publicists and marketing people who will do all of this for you.

Keep in mind; a publisher will promote your book for a short amount of time. If it doesn't catch on, chances are you won't get another book deal. You won't be able to self-promote it. A family friend published with one of the big five. He has less than ten reviews, all suspiciously the input of family and friends. The more you understand reviews, you will recognize a bogus one and realize everyone else can spot them too. His book had perhaps a month of publicity. Yes, he made it on a few morning shows, did a book signing, and had a few high-end parties in

Manhattan. When the book failed in the ratings, it was abandoned. He was not allowed to do anything without their consent or approval. It fizzled along with his career in writing.

2 - Paid Publishers

It is difficult to get signed by a publisher, and that is why independent publishing is booming. Be aware that there are independent publishers that you have to pay to publish your book. People do this all the time because they aren't sure how to get published on their own.

Books get published, and promises are made. Quality may not be an issue, and usually, neither is promoting the book. There are a lot of unhappy people with stories to tell about these experiences. Google every company you are considering. Read the reviews. There are reputable companies out there, but it is up to you to find them.

"Vanity" publishers do not have strict selection processes when it comes to accepting a manuscript. Some will accept a book although the quality of writing is lousy. Editing isn't a priority with some, and many times, they publish books riddled with errors. Some do this while charging you exorbitant fees. Thousands of dollars change hands. Unfortunately, it's money going out of the writer's pockets and into the publisher's hands.

These publishers are still out there. New writers may not understand the difference between these publishers and traditional publishers. Be aware that there are big differences. If your book is good and you don't want to wait on a traditional publishing house to accept you, you have other options. Google is your friend. Research and find out more about any company before you sign a contract or money exchanges hands.

Self-publishing is relatively easy. There are several sites where all you have to do is load your manuscript, have it formatted, purchase a cover, and publish. There are also other perks to self-publishing. Upper management and the guys wearing the suits will not constrain you. Sometimes writing a book is a vanity project; other times it's highly subjective or personal. Publishers may shy away from these subjects. To a publisher, the bottom line is always profit, not necessarily yours either. Once you involve a publisher, you may lose creative and financial control. You may have to tweak your work to fit their ideals. There are pros and cons to both sides of this coin.

Certainly, shopping a manuscript or idea with publishers defrays the cost and energy to publicize your book once it is published. There are a lot of new presses out there. Make sure to have an attorney read any contract you are considering. Some authors want a publisher; others enjoy the freedom of being their own boss.

Carole's Experience

Thirty years ago, I wrote a little steamy romance and worked with one of these types of publishing houses under a different name. I paid almost ten thousand dollars to have it produced. It pops up on Amazon if you search for it. I think I sold one copy, maybe two. All the publicity and promotion was up to me. I knew nothing about any of this type of work. This was before the years of the internet or social marketing.

My takeaway was that if you want to sell a self-published book, be prepared to take on every aspect of its promotion. Roll up your sleeves with the understanding that this cannot be a part-time venture. It will suck the life from you more than your emotional novel. However, it can be worth it if you are willing to invest the time.

3 - No Fee Publishers

There are a few small, independent publishers out there that do not require agents to submit your book. Another plus? They won't charge you either. One of the newer companies, TopShelf Indie Authors & Books (Julie likes what they offer authors so much she now has a stake in the company) will allow you to submit a sample of your book for consideration. A few others I've found that seem to be traditional publishers are Turner Publishing and Mountain Press Publishing

Company. If your book is a good fit and does well, some publishing companies will give you an advance on future books.

Be sure to follow rules and guidelines for submitting your books if you decide to forgo self-publishing. Some publishers will only accept scholarly books, while others may only want children's books. Take the time to read their online websites.

4 - Self-Publishing Print on Demand

Dozens of new companies are popping up all over the internet that allow an author to download their book and instantly publish it. They offer a variety of services, including publishing e-books, as well as paperbacks, and in some cases hardcovers. They are called POD or "print on demand." There is no need to print books in advance, taking the chance that they may not be sold and end up languishing in a stockroom.

You are given choices when it comes to the size of your book, paper type, and color, and if you want a matte or glossy cover. Books are ordered at major retailers like Amazon or Barnes & Noble, and these sites print them as they are purchased. Some of these companies are Createspace, Lulu, and Bookbaby.com to name a few.

You can choose to make your book accessible to mass distribution as well. Though the profit margin is small, you want your books in every library and bookstore, as well as big-box stores like Target and Walmart.

IngramSpark.com offers publishing services too. With a small setup fee, they can get your book in the hands of people worldwide. They network with over forty thousand retailers and librarians across the globe and offer both digital and print distribution options.

If you have chosen to go the self-publishing house route, try to find one that will give you the most freedom as well as offer the most services. Search the internet, check reviews, and make sure they are trustworthy.

Carole's Experience with POD

As newbies, we found Createspace gave us the most options. They did our first covers. They connected us with the illustrators that helped me shape my children's books. They had a department for everything from making a video about the book to marketing plans. We found them to be a terrific one-stop shopping center.

However, as time passed, they closed down many of these services. After a moment of panic, we realized we could do it all on our own, and now we shall share our vast store of experience.

I worked with another self-publishing service that came highly recommended and turned out to be disorganized. The sales representatives did not know their product. I was specific about the services I had to have and which ones I did not. They assured me that I was getting what I needed. They charged me about twenty-five hundred dollars for a package, advising me that I needed a custom order to have my hardcover books sized accurately.

Needless to say, there was a flurry of emails, and when they didn't get back to me promptly, I started to get worried. It seems the person I had spoken to was fired; the right hand didn't know what the left hand was doing. All of a sudden, they couldn't provide me with the services I was assured they had. Nobody seemed to have a detailed record of our first call.

Nobody - except for me. I kept precise notes of all the dates of our discussions and with whom I had spoken. I explained they were charging me a crazy amount of money for services I was getting for free at Createspace. A few tense days followed when I didn't know if I would get back my deposit. Be sure you keep accurate records of whom you speak to and make sure you know exactly what you need before you sign a contract for their services.

Most companies will give you a publishing consultant and a team who will walk you through each step of the process. Many offer services from cover art to editorial, and some include a press release for you to send out.

5 - Self-Published E-book

E-book publishing has been on the rise. It's easy and quick, and many authors are growing an e-book publishing empire. The "e" in e-book stands for electronic. It's the book you read on your Kindle or Nook. You can carry your books everywhere you go, and when you finish one, there is always a new book waiting. If you don't have an e-reader, there's an app that you can download to make it possible to read e-books on any electronic device. These book versions are easy to store on your device or in the Cloud. No need to make room on the bookshelf, which is ideal for a book hoarder like me.

You can publish e-books through Amazon's KDP (Kindle) site. The process is simple. This e-book was published using KDP. Start with a formatted file and upload your book and cover. Fill out a little information on your book and choose categories to make it easier for people to find your book online.

Remember, there are many POD, independent, and small time publishers that can easily be found online. Research any of the companies that you are considering. There are a lot of publishing companies that will publish your book, but authors have had to fend for themselves when it comes to promoting them because those publishing companies fall flat with that end of the deal. The good thing about authors is that they have a tendency to write about their experiences in forums and blogs. They may also write about their experiences on Yelp.com or other review sites. If you want to know the truth about a company, it's out there. Find it!

To Do List:

1 - Research publishing options.
2 - Choose a publisher based on your needs and abilities to promote your book.

3 - Pick what kind of book you want to publish - e-book, softcover, or hardcover - and where you want to see it distributed.

4 - Start researching ways to promote your book.

CHAPTER 6

IT ISN'T THE SIZE OF YOUR DESCRIPTION; IT'S HOW YOU USE IT
~ JULIE AND CAROLE

Now it's time to put together your pitch for the back of the book. The little blurb you write will play multiple roles. It will be next to or underneath the image of the book where it is sold on the internet. It will be what people read when they look up your book on Goodreads. It will probably be in your publicity release and on the information sheets you are sending out to bookstore buyers and reviewers. The only thing I can compare it to is trying to squeeze ten pounds of crap into a two-pound bag!

Writing a book description seems like an easy thing to do. It can be intimidating, considering it is your first official ad for your book. You are selling your book to the masses, and your description is essential to the book's success.

Set the scene and use words that create a mood. Is your book funny or dark and mysterious? Don't talk about subplots or minor characters, instead keep with the main ones. Try to avoid referring to "the book" and using terminology like "readers." Don't use words like "you" or "I." Write in a third person narrative.

It's also important to avoid those typical clichés that some authors like to use. It makes it sound as if they are trying to sell something in an infomercial, like when they are referring to the book as "the book to own," "must read," or "must have." If you refer to your book, add the name in italics as all book titles should be. It's okay to use short lines of praise or quotes about your book from other authors. If Stephen King or Nicholas Sparks mentions my book, you better believe I am going to use it.

If you want to compare the book to other well-known books or authors, don't be afraid to do so; make sure you aren't misleading readers. Tease your readers with a few hints of what's to come. Your description is the foreplay that will either get everyone revved up and excited to read your book or turn them off completely. Make sure you do it right.

Think of the book description as your first ad. It should be short, attention grabbing, and sell the book using the first line. Give them enough, so they understand what the book is about, but remember, just a tease. Don't give away the ending, and please don't summarize the book. Break it down into multiple, short paragraphs instead of one long one because it makes your description easier to read.

My sons and I usually do this part together. We try to describe the book in less than four sentences. Michael calls it an elevator pitch. You have to pitch your book in the same amount of time it takes to ride the elevator to the sixth floor. Having these restrictions keeps the descriptions of our books brief and deliciously appetizing.

You will have to put this pitch on the description page when you upload your book to most sites, along with a current photo and a short biography.

If you type Google Word Count into your search bar or go to WordCounter.net, you can use the tool to find the count of the characters as well as the number of words in a document. Try using different sentence combinations to give an idea of how many words you'll have in the description. If you use Google Drive, you will find "Tools" near the top of the page, and it will give you the count information. The ideal length of your description is anywhere from eighty to two hundred words. I recommend keeping the novel within the pages and not adding it to the back cover.

We like to keep the description to about three paragraphs, one that introduces the protagonist, the second paragraph is the character's goal, and the last part is about who is in their way or trying to stop them. It's the *takeaway promise* of the book.

Here are some examples:

The Flip by Michael Phillip Cash

Julie and Brad Evans are house flippers. (Introduction to the main characters.)

They buy low, clean out the old occupants' junk, and try to make a profit. (The goal or mission.)

Enter Hemmings House on Bedlam Street in scenic Cold Spring Harbor. It's too good a deal to pass up but with an ominous secret. The old Victorian mansion has dwellers that do not want to be dispossessed. As the house reveals its past, will the couple's marriage survive The Flip? (The obstacle that will block their path creating the drama about to unfold.)

The After House by Michael Phillip Cash

After having failed marriages, Remy Galway and her daughter, Olivia, are rebuilding their lives in a three-hundred-year-old cottage in historic Cold Spring Harbor, Long Island. (Combined protagonist and mission. They need to set up a new life for themselves and return to normalcy.)

Little do they know, another occupant is lurking in the haven of their home. Will the After House be their shelter or their tomb? (This shows obstacle as well as a creepy tone. It also concentrates on the heart of the book, letting the reader know it could be an epic fight to the death.)

Being a Captain Is Hard Work by Carole P. Roman

Writing the description for a children's book is hard work. You are appealing to two audiences. You have to give enough for the parents to want to share the book with their children, yet it has to be engaging to your target audience as well.

Captain No Beard is determined to travel to Dew Rite Volcano. (The introduction.)

He won't listen when Mongo predicts a storm or Linus indicates they are headed in the wrong direction. He insists Polly cook in the galley although the seas are getting rough. What's a crew to do with a stubborn, know-it-all captain? (The obstacle. I know, you're supposed to mention one main character, but this book is part of a series, and all the characters play a significant role.)

Will they convince the captain he is barreling headlong into danger, or will Captain No Beard jeopardize both his safety and the crew's with his single-minded determination to go where he wants?" (This goal tells their parents there will be a valuable lesson in the story.)

Tortured Souls: The House On Wellfleet Bluffs by Linda Cadose, J.A.Gerber, M.M. Hudson

In some towns, the past is easily forgotten. Not in Wellfleet Bluffs. Lynne and Jason buy their dream house online and quickly move to the quaint little town. (The introduction of the main characters - can't you envision dark, moody skies?)

After unexplained events send them looking for answers, will they become a forgotten part of history or will they find the answers and help the ghosts of the past find peace? (The promise of the premise - will the main characters get lost in the past too?)

The Lucidites (3 Book Series) by Sarah Noffke

Around the world, humans are hallucinating after sleepless nights. In a sterile, underground institute, the forecasters keep reporting the same events. In the backwoods of Texas, a sixteen-year-old girl is about to be caught up in a fierce, ethereal battle. (Setting the mood - letting the reader know this is a book not of our world.)

Meet Roya Stark. She drowns every night in her dreams, spends her hours reading classic literature to avoid her family's ridicule, and is prone to premonitions—which are becoming more frequent. Now the dreams are filled with strangers offering to reveal what she has always wanted to know: Who is she? (Introducing the main character and revealing her goals.)

That's the question that haunts her, and she's about to find out. But will Roya live to regret learning the truth? (The truth is her obstacle.)

All of these books have spent time in the top one hundred slot of the genre on Amazon. Some of them for a considerable amount of time. Each one of these writers described their books differently. They all set a tone, introduced the characters to watch, didn't give away the story, and best of all, made the reader open the book.

Using minimal language, they conveyed what Blake Snyder called the *promise of the premise* or the heart and soul of their books.

Silverton County SD-101: Good Choices by C.P. Duhart

There have always been wolves. (Sounds ominous. Sets the mood for the book.)

Creeping and prowling at the edges of the places we think are safe, they remind us the world can be more frightening than we care to admit. They survive by being the worst type of predators we can imagine: predators that are clever enough to learn our moves and patient enough to strike when we least expect it. And as much as we may think our campfires keep us safe, we still feel their eyes on us from the darkness - waiting for a single moment of inattention. Until someone forgets the unfortunate reasons we avoid the dark. (Dark, elicits feelings of fear. I am expecting predators from society that are waiting for the right moment to attack. This is the goal, we must avoid the dark or risk the unknown.)

Yes, there have always been wolves. There will always be wolves. But what happens when the wolves are no longer waiting at the edge of darkness, biding their time? What happens when wolves meet you at your front door? (This gives me an idea of what to expect when I read the book. There is going to be conflict or obstacle, and the way the author describes it, I am curious.)

As you can see, there are many ways to put together a vivid book description. Find more examples by browsing sites like Amazon and Goodreads. Some authors can write one in a matter of minutes, and sometimes it takes days to put one together. Take your time and think about how you want to sell your book.

The Liahona Effect (A Michael DiBianco Novel) by Keith Katsikas

THE NEWTON PROPHECIES is a lightening-fast thriller, following Harvard Divinity professor, Michael DiBianco across three countries, on a life-and-death mission to thwart a plot of terror the likes of which the world has never before seen, only to discover a dark secret about his past that could ultimately spawn the apocalypse. (Here the author accomplishes everything in one sentence. He has introduced his MC (main character), stated his goal, and ends with the obstacle, the threat of an apocalypse.)

Now that you have a description of the book, you should prepare a media release or press release. This is a letter of introduction for your book. It should have the book's description, relevant information like the ISBN, the price, where it can be purchased, your bio, and a picture of the cover, as well as yourself.

You can include a list of your other work to remind them of earlier books. Include the sheet whenever you send the books to anyone. They can be printed at any printing store like a Staples.

Carole P. Roman

Children's Book Author

If You Were Me And Lived In... Egypt

This exciting and informative new children's series, "If You Were Me and Lived in..." takes young readers on worldwide tour of different countries and their cultures.

Book Summary:
Join Carole P. Roman when she visits the stunning and exciting land of Egypt in the newest book of her informative series. Learn why this ancient land often called "the cradle of civilization." Travel down the Nile to discover Egypt's fascinating history. See the land through the eyes of a youngster like you and understand what life is like in this exotic place.

Don't forget to look at the other books in the series so that you can be an armchair world traveler.

For Purchase:
www.caroleproman.com
www.amazon.com
(Reviews are welcome on amazon!)

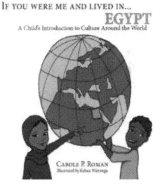

About Carole:

Award winning author Carole P. Roman is a former teacher turned businesswoman. She has successfully run a family business with her husband. Her most favorite job is being grandmother to her many grandchildren. She currently lives on Long Island with her husband.

Her first book, "Captain No Beard - An Imaginary Tale of a Pirate's Life" has been named to Kirkus Reviews' Best of 2012 as well garnered the star of remarkable merit. Three more Captain No Beard books are in the works. Also available, "I Want To Do Yoga Too," a children's introduction to yoga.

To Do List:

1 - Write your book description, keeping in mind it is the first thing that people will read and will determine whether they buy your book.

2 - Prepare a press release sheet filled with information about your book and where it can be purchased.

CHAPTER 7

BIOS - GETTING TO KNOW YOU
~ CAROLE AND JULIE

I froze like a deer in the headlights the first time I had to write my biography. My consultant at Createspace said, "Pretend you are writing about someone else."

Why should anyone read your book? What makes your story better than the nine million other books on Amazon or Barnes & Noble? Are you an expert, former Marine, perhaps a teacher, or a Taekwondo master? What one or two details in your life set you apart from the crowd?

My books are geared for children, my nonfiction series for students, so I always begin with the words "award-winning" or "former teacher." This lets people know I am in my area of expertise. Mentioning your awards never hurts either.

People like to see what the author looks like, so take a nice photo. You will have to load it on Amazon and for every blog post that writes an article about you. We have several different shots, each done with our cell phone. Remember, if you use someone else's (a professional) photo, you must give them credit.

Both my son and I asked an illustrator to do a picture. It was a fun alternative on the back of his book. For me, I used it in both blog posts and for advertising.

This bio is from one of my cultural nonfiction series.

Award-winning author, Carole P. Roman, is delighted to add India to her growing series. She is currently completing *If You Were Me and Lived in...Portugal, Greece, and Russia,* which she researched and wrote with her five-year-old grandson, Alexander. Her first book, *Captain No Beard: An Imaginary Tale of a Pirate's Life,* was named as Kirkus Best of 2012, received the Star of Remarkable Merit, the Pinnacle Award for 2012, and recently, the Erik Metzroth Award for Best Children's Book 2013.

Here is a nonfiction, self-help book. The author opens his bio with his credentials. Next, he declares why he wrote this book. He explains how he qualifies the information and closes by stating where he lives.

With degrees in English and Finance along with a Master of Business Administration degree, Michael Samuels has attracted everything into his life because he followed successful people and their thought processes. He has read and thoroughly tested hundreds of books on spirituality, self-improvement, and the metaphysical. The Universe has helped Michael run a highly successful family-owned business with offices all over the country. He currently lives in New York with his wife and son. *Just Ask the Universe* is his first book.

This one is for one of my pirate books. Notice I mention as many of my series as I can. If the readers like this one, perhaps they'll search for others.

Carole P. Roman is the award-winning author of the *Captain No Beard* series. Both *Captain No Beard: An Imaginary Tale of a Pirate's Life* and *Captain No Beard and the Aurora Borealis* have received the Kirkus Star of Exceptional Merit. The first book in the series was named as Kirkus Reviews' Best 2012. *Captain No Beard and the Aurora Borealis* was recently named as Kirkus Reviews' Best of 2015. Each book in the series has won numerous awards including the NABE Pinnacle Award, ERIK Award for 2013, Foreword Reviews Five Star, a Finalist in the

Book of the Year, and Reader's Views Children's Book of the Year 2013. Roman is also the author of the award-winning nonfiction culture series *If You Were Me and Lived in*...exploring customs and culture around the world.

One of my son's books. We added his social media information at the bottom, along with a list of all his books.

Michael Phillip Cash is an award-winning screenwriter and novelist. He attended the Long Island University and used its beautiful campus as a backdrop for this novel. He has written eleven novels including the best-selling *Brood X, Stillwell, The Flip, The After House, Witches Protection Program,* and *Monsterland.*

Michael resides on the North Shore of Long Island with his wife and two children.

Connect with Michael on:
Facebook: facebook.com/michaelphillipcash
Twitter: twitter.com/michaelpcash
Web: www.michaelphillipcash.com
Email: michaelphillipcash@gmail.com

Sarah wrote a short biography that nails the main points. She lists the link to her newsletter in the last line to gain new fans. It is important to put your links out there so fans won't have to track you down like a bill collector. Make it easy for them.

Sarah Noffke writes YA and NA sci-fi fantasy and is the author of *The Lucidites, Reverians, Ren,* and *Vagabond Circus* series. She holds a Master of Management and teaches college business courses. Most of her students have no idea that she toils away her hours crafting fictional characters. Noffke's books are top-rated and best-sellers on Kindle. Currently, she has eleven novels published. Her books are available in paperback, audio, and Spanish and Italian.

To stay up to date with Sarah, please subscribe to her newsletter: http://www.sarahnoffke.com/connect

Don't be afraid to have some fun and let your personality shine. I've seen plenty of biographies out there that made me want to follow the author to get an occasional dose of humor when those newsletters arrive in my inbox. They were entirely different, grabbed my attention immediately, and made me smile, like Mandie Stevens's bio.

Mandie Stevens has always been accused of living in her own world, so she decided to put it to paper. When she isn't writing, you can catch her lounging on the beach reading. Mandie has penned both nonfiction and urban fantasy.

She has ridiculously little feet and would be happy eating seafood every day.

Look around and read other examples on Amazon or other sites and show people who you are. You could always use this as an opportunity to reinvent yourself!

To Do List:

1 - **Prepare your biography. You will need it. Anyone who promotes your books will want to tell their readers about you.**
2 - **Have someone take a picture or have one professionally done to be used for the back of your book, blog posts, and articles.**

CHAPTER 8

COVER STORY ~ CAROLE AND JULIE

Okay, we have a finished product, so it's time to publish, right? The beta reader likes it; your spouse is impressed. The kids think you are amazing, and your mother-in-law is talking about your budding talent at Mah Jong. Zip over to Createspace, Lulu, TopShelf Publishing, or Bookbaby.com, and we're off! *New York Times* here we come.

Wait a second there, cowboy. We are nowhere ready to be found in print. Your book is not dressed. You have no cover. It's like you sent your book out in public naked. What were you thinking?

The cover is the first impression. It has to entice readers, invite them, and stir up interest. It's the eye-candy that makes them stop their speedy perusal of titles and makes them think, *Hmm, I might like that.* There are several ways to do it. Your cover will tell a story of its own, and you should make sure it matches the story inside. Remember to get the exact dimensions and size of your book before you begin. You will need it for creating the cover.

There are thousands of premade covers on the internet waiting to be picked. You can search by genre, or if you are looking for a particular element to feature on the cover, you can use that keyword in your search. After adding keywords, like house, fog, or any element you want to include, you'll have entire collections to sift through until you find the one you want.

Premade covers are inexpensive if you are on a tight budg
new authors. If you find one you can't live without, grab it
someone else does. They usually won't duplicate covers so
could be one-of-a-kind. Be sure to confirm that before maki
purchase. Decide if you are publishing an e-book or paperback or both.
With some designers, you will need to buy both formats for your book.

An example of a premade cover. We chose the cover because of the
image, which was how we envisioned the backdrop of the house in the
book. The story is multilayered, and about so much more than just a
house. It's moody, shifting, and the main characters are on uncertain
ground.

f you want to go all out, have someone create a custom cover. You describe the key elements and mood of your books.

99Designs.com is a site found on the web that can create custom covers. They can cost anywhere from five hundred to a thousand dollars for the right-looking cover. Another choice is Ampersand Book Covers on Etsy who will sell you a premade cover for a few hundred dollars or work with you to create a custom cover for a fair price. Cover Quill is another helpful site.

Some authors prefer to design their covers by working only through email with an artist. If you are going without the umbrella of one of these companies, make sure you have the legal rights to reproduce and use the cover for all your needs. Have a lawyer draw up a contract.

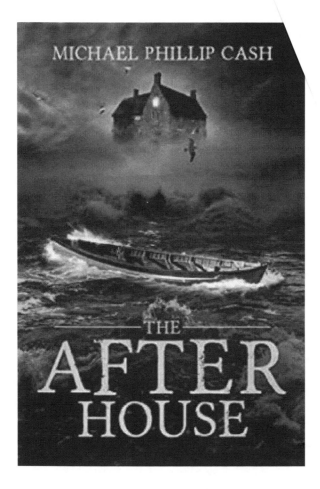

We received feedback because some readers said this cover didn't reflect the inside of the book. The book had a humorous element mixed with ghosts. They expected a more frightening book from the illustration. We liked it and have decided not to change it.

Creating your cover is achieved by listing what you think you might like on the front and back, colors, and describing the genre. With a company like 99Designs, artists bid on the work. Several artists respond, and you choose the designer that you feel suits your book. He or she submits three different designs, and you pick the one that will work.

ike using these type of services. They protect your rights with the artwork. You certainly don't want to get into a legal battle with an artist who decides they want their cover back after you've published. You can do what you want with the images, and your deal is finished with the artist. If you decide to print posters and show them everywhere, you can do that. If a studio buys the rights to your book and uses the cover, they only need your permission.

A custom cover. Lives flipped by the events in the story. The present reflecting on the past. A haunting story. The cover represented the story perfectly.

If you want to design your cover, you can purchase stock ʌ
and edit them to show your title and name. On some of thes
can purchase an image with a standard license for under forty
Use a company like IStockPhoto, Shutterstock, or Getty Imagɩ   ʌse
they give you freedom from legal responsibility if you follow thɩʌr terms
of use. It's a nice insurance to have.

There is one huge issue with using stock photos for your book cover.
Other authors will have access to the same cover. The title and author's
name will differ, but your cover art will not be exclusive to you if
someone else makes the same purchase. If you want something that no
one else has, look into premade or custom covers, just be sure they won't
sell the identical cover to anyone else before you make your purchase.

You will also need to make sure you purchase the correct licensing and
buy the extended license for paperback printing if needed. You should
read the fine print. Some licenses can be revoked without warning.
In those cases, you will need to find, create, and load another cover
immediately.

You can also use personal photos. Remember, if you use someone's
photograph (like a friend), you have to have written permission. If you
decide to purchase a photo, make sure that you buy a license to use that
image more than once. This rule applies to any photo you use for your
book or promotions. If you find it online, it doesn't mean it's free.

Some cover designers will want your book's final page count (which
you will have after the book is correctly formatted) to complete the
paperback and spine artwork. They will also want to know the size of
your book and your book description for the back cover if you need a
paperback book cover. The cover will grab the attention of readers. The
description will seal the deal.

Credit: Laura Hidalgo at Bookfabulous Designs

Once you've chosen the artist that best represents what you want, he or she designs one that will sell your book. Judging a book by its cover happens every day in Indieworld.

Whatever you do, please don't upload an old photograph and write your title and name somewhere on it and think you are going to make tons of money from sales. If you love books and read a lot, you've seen those covers. Make good choices. You don't want to end up on lousybookcovers.com or covercritics.com. There are also awards for best covers, so it's nice to be recognized for the cost and effort.

To Do List:

1 - Prepare a budget and then choose a cover to fit your book.

CHAPTER 9

ARTWORK - COLOR YOUR WORLD AND EVERYONE ELSE'S ~ CAROLE

You must protect yourself with a contract if you work with an artist for illustrations for a project like a children's book. I have collaborated with illustrators directly employed by the self-publishing company. I was under their umbrella regarding ownership of the images in my children's books, but when they phased out the artists, I contacted the artists directly and worked out an agreement.

I made sure the artists signed a contract with me, giving me the exclusive rights to the illustrations and characters. I had a copyright lawyer make a generic contract that has pesky information like my ownership, deadlines, and payments. This protects both the artist and myself. There are no gray areas. I set up a payment schedule, and the funds were released according to the milestones we reached. I have paid anywhere from thirty to one hundred and fifty dollars for an illustration.

Money is held in escrow when you work with one of these companies. You release the funds as they complete portions of the job. If you decide to work directly with an artist, payment is easily made through PayPal.

An artist has to know the correct size of your book. You'll have to choose fonts and colors for the text. They need the ISBN (International Standard Book Number) and any other identification. I usually send a screenshot directly from my Createspace page, so I don't mess up information.

The author sends a list of how many images and the subject of each one. It's harder than you think. You have lived with the characters in your head. They have quirks that are real to you; you must convey what you need to be shown to a complete stranger who may only give the design a few hours in their busy day. Yes, they have lives and other projects too. It's important you don't let them take over your characters with their perceptions.

You'll have to describe hair color, ethnicity, facial features, clothing, etc. - you name it. You can't imagine all the details you have to move from your head, where you take it for granted, to another person to translate to paper. You'd be surprised at the results.

Your artist will send sketches first, like a storyboard to see if he or she has captured what you are trying to say in your text. Now is the time for changes. Look for the details, and read your text to see if it matches what you are saying.

Obviously, you can't have an illustration for every sentence if you have more than a few lines on each page. Also, understand that the cost of your project will go up as you add artwork. I try to lay out the text in an action grouping, stressing to the artist what should be highlighted in the picture.

For instance, in my Captain No Beard series, if Polly the parrot is supposed to be giving out pretzels to Linus, the lion, don't approve a picture of her holding a juice cup and Mongo the monkey dancing around it. It has to match the action.

If I am working with a group of sentences, I tell the artist to highlight the most meaningful action, trying to include all the characters involved in that portion of the text. Many times one character is left out, so if I had Captain No Beard giving a direction to Linus, who is nowhere in sight, I might switch the text to reflect that he is talking to another character who is available. Sometimes this is impossible, and the artist will have to redo the illustration. I try to respect their time and work with them to be quick and efficient.

As you have preconceived notions of how an illustration should be done, so does the artist. Very often there can be a charge when altering an illustration, so be as descriptive as you can when giving the information.

One artist explained it to me like this; an artist has to select the most interesting and dynamic moment while including all the details. When they read the manuscript, unless you tell them the entire backstory, they will miss many of those things.

Consider an artist reading the following text.

> *Molly was angry. Her mother told her that she couldn't have any more cookies. She caught her red-handed in the cookie jar.*
> *Molly stormed out of the house, kicking the watering can as she stomped along.*
> *When she got to the fence gate at the house, she had an idea. "I'll show her. I'm going to run away. That way I can eat all the cookies I want!"*
> *She looked at her red bicycle propped against the gate after throwing a last angry glare toward the house. She hopped on her bike, then took off, speeding toward the woods.*

An illustrator would choose to draw Molly speeding off on her bike out of the frame of the picture. However, she may include more details in the background. This may be the rendition the artist illustrates:

> *The house includes a nearby fence; her mother is on the porch, wagging her finger at Molly. An empty cookie jar is tucked under the mother's arm, or there is an image of the mother with her hands on her hips with an angry expression. The watering can is knocked over in a puddle. Molly will be glaring back at the house while riding off, (although she gave a look first then hopped on her bike).*

In one illustration, the artist captures everything that occurred, although the action happened in three different places: the kitchen, front yard, and leaving the yard.

Since I write fiction as well as nonfiction, I have been lucky enough to work with the best in the business. Bonnie Lemaire embraced my Captain No Beard series like a mother hen. She captured the antics of the kids with her delightful, whimsical drawings. This was a personal project for me. The subjects are my family and each time I opened her email, I was floored by her insights.

The artist didn't know the characters were my grandkids and was never given a picture; her ability to read between the lines was uncanny! It's a beautiful series and dear to my heart.

I chose Kelsea Wierenga to do my first nonfiction series. I loved her style. I explained in our first email that I wanted respectful and not cliché images. She jumped aboard, researching with incredible accuracy. She is tireless and has become my creative consultant on everything I do.

Kelsea understood these books were aimed at young ones as an introduction to customs and culture around the world. The proof of her dedication is seen on the awards dotting the covers of the series. *If You Were Me and Lived in...* has grown to over nineteen books at this printing. They sell well and have a broad appeal.

The artists have learned to be patient with me too. In the past, I contracted for fifteen images to save money. As the book progressed, I realized I needed more illustrations. I learned you couldn't crowd the text page with five actions and only show one. Kids and their parents have high expectations and will let you know loud and clear. Sometimes, I will change my text rather than alter the image for a smoother feel. As I said before, some artists will charge additionally for changing an illustration, or reworking the dialog. Make sure you know his or her policy before you begin.

Color images come next, and that is a happy day. Your characters jump off the pages, and your mind spins with ideas for coloring books, tee shirts, and stuffed animals. It's fun-and-games time.

Next is the tedious job of matching the text to the illustrations. This has taken me longer than writing the books in some cases. Here is where you must move things around so they will appear on the correct page; actions should reflect the text. It is extremely frustrating. I am close enough to the talented people I work with to ask their opinion. They have an understanding of space and design that eludes me. I usually yield to their judgment.

The illustrators should know how to format. They send you a completed file, ready to upload. I use Dropbox and PDFs in my email. Dropbox is a communal storage site where your projects are delivered for you to download onto your computer.

You think you're done yet? Not by a longshot. Somehow the text is all wrong. Words were lost; sentences are fractured. You have to go through each page, fixing where the text is incorrect or doesn't work and needs a change.

When you write the artist the corrections, include the page number as well as the line number from the top of the page where the text is in trouble. You should copy and paste exactly what's there, then rewrite the text as it should be. This can take forever, especially if there is a language barrier or when your artist lives in another time zone.

Illustrators are trained not to read the copy so that they won't interfere with the story. If you make a mistake, they will copy your mistake.

In the end, I think it's all magic if you ask me. I learned to press the appropriate buttons on the various programs but have experienced numerous panic attacks when something didn't work or disappeared. Fortunately, my kids live nearby, and I trade computer troubleshooting with babysitting. I think it's a good deal, and clearly, I am the winner!

When I started writing, these things were vague applications. I will admit I still don't know much about them and depend on the illustrators to be able to tell me where and what to do. I have asked Kelsea to explain some of the mediums they use. I have no idea; I choose what appeals to me.

Kelsea indicated artwork is split into two varieties: tradition and digital illustrations.
Traditional mediums include painting, watercolor, acrylic, and oil. There are pen and ink or pastels, which is chalk. The artist takes the image and scans it to place in the book digitally. I know Bonnie uses watercolors, and I have bought many of the original paintings.

Digital mediums are Raster pixel-based programs like Adobe Photoshop, which makes digital paintings. Photoshop uses photo manipulation where the work is photographically based or based on a drawing. Styles include painterly, whimsical, pattern, heavy texture, sketchy lines, and hand-rendered qualities.

In vector-based programs like Adobe Illustrator, artworks have elements filled with color, blends, tints, or gradients and are not photographic or drawing based. The styles include pop art, logo-type, and "cartoonish rendering of characters."

Five Key Questions to Ask an Illustrator:

1 - Determine the type of business agreement before you start. Some illustrators want to "partner" in your book project, sharing both the cost and distribution cost as well as sharing the profits from the royalties and having equal ownership.

Some are willing to take a flat fee, with the author making all the decisions. The author collects one hundred percent of the profits. Either way, make sure you have a written contract with these issues clearly defined.

2 - Ask your illustrator if they are familiar with self-publishing. Even though many have formal degrees in art, they may only know about traditional publishing. They need to understand there will not be a ten

thousand print book run; there won't be payment in advance on the project, and it moves at a fast pace.

The average time to complete the illustrations in traditional publishing is about one year. A self-publishing project can take as little as two months. It varies with each author.

3 - Ask if they are familiar with the assorted mediums and styles. Pick your artist based on his capabilities in that style. In your interview, use descriptions like "painterly" or "photo-realistic," depending on your vision of your book.

Stress what is important to you such as detailed backgrounds or beautiful landscapes, knowledge about an individual concept, and readable character expressions.

4 - Make sure you understand the process of illustration changes throughout the project. It's important to know at what point an artist will charge a fee to make a change to an illustration.

5 - Figure out a good way to communicate with your artist. Do you need to see every stage of the process from storyboard to completion or only the finished product?

I have used Upwork.com for illustrations when looking for artists for some of my other children's books. I love to use assorted styles and themes, depending on the age group. On Upwork, there is a community of thousands of different artists from all over the world. They provide samples and have a list of comments; you can pick someone you think will do the job. Once you've posted the requirements for your project, you choose an artist that you think will work best with your subject by looking at their samples.

Your satisfaction is important to the Upwork team, and there are many ways to contact the right people if the job is not working out. I didn't have that problem, so I can't tell you the response if you are not satisfied.

I liked working with them because the contracts of Upwork protect me. Upwork is clear that you are the owner of all the images created once you've paid for them. They cannot be used or reproduced without your permission. This ensures that I own all the rights to the artwork and can do whatever I want with the images. For instance, if I sell my characters to a studio for a movie, I own them, and they only have to negotiate with me, not with the artist too.

It's important to use the right type of artist for your work, and keeping them on a reasonable schedule makes for a happier experience. I don't bug them to finish, and they know they will get more work when they adhere to the agreement. We do lay out our expectations in an email, so we both have a basic idea of our timeline.

Any artist you work with must know how to format a book for publication. I have collaborated with many artists who assured me that they understood how to prepare a book ready to be loaded onto a site like Createspace.

One time they didn't, and for that matter, neither did I. It was aggravating. I am not technical in that way. I ended up asking Kelsea to take over and format, so the work was done effortlessly. Once you are comfortable with someone and their style, it is hard to start with new people.

I have hired additional artists I found on the internet, who mastered the skill of both formatting and delivery, producing products ready to be loaded without an issue. That has worked well too. They took the time to contact Createspace and learn how to do it properly and in response to their dedication, I have given them additional work.
You can find one illustrator that will represent your characters and your style. Many people do that. You have to look at certain books, and from the illustrations, you will know who the author is. It becomes part of their brand.

Bonnie is the only artist I would hire to work the *Captain No Beard* series. The characters are the icons of that story, and I wouldn't mess with its success. Kelsea has done a marvelous job on the cultural series, and I wanted to make sure each book started out on the same playing field. The idea was to have kids not think any country is better or worse due to the images. My intent to show our global connection stays true to my theme.

While some critics complained of the sameness of the illustrations in that series, I decided to hire many illustrators from all over the world for a feeling of diversity for my newest project. We are exploring time periods throughout history. Traveling to various civilizations, each book is to be different looking. However, Kelsea remains on board to make sure the elements stay true to the mission of the series. I think we have succeeded in this goal.

One problem I ran into was with illustrations for the children's books in my series. I always checked the internet to see if any of my books were mentioned on blogs or articles. My main character was hijacked. I found someone trying to trademark him. I had to hire a lawyer to prevent the trademark from succeeding.

To Do List:

1 - **Decide which medium you want to use for your artwork if your book requires it.**
2 - **Pick an artist from a reputable source.**
3 - **If you are working without the benefit of going through a company, make sure you have a proper contract that protects your rights to the illustrations and characters.**
4 - **Make sure the actions in the illustrations match the text on each page.**
5 - **Verify that the artist knows what you need technically to load your book.**

CHAPTER 10
BOOK TRAILERS ~ JULIE

Book trailers aren't vital to your success, but they are another creative way to add a little cinematic drama to your promotions. Who doesn't like movies? Some trailers are done so well that they alone have made me purchase a book.

We use LoewenHerz-Creative. They have always done a fantastic job combining elements to bring some life into the books we select for trailers. Keep in mind that they can take a couple of months to create. Put your order in early if you want to release the trailer before your actual book launch. Book trailer prices can be affordable, but you will need to look around. We have paid a little over one hundred dollars, but some companies charge over five hundred for a professional video.

There are other companies out there that will put together trailers for your book. You can find freelancers on fiverr, and if you search for book trailers, you will come up with dozens of affordable options. You can find a lot of professional services on this site if you search.

You can find resources online that will walk you through making your own. Before you buy, check out the company or individual's portfolio of trailers and decide if they have that edge you are looking for, then load your video onto Youtube or use it on your website and Facebook page.

If you choose to create your book trailer, sites like ANIMOTO. com will give you everything you need to produce slideshows and professional-looking videos. You can choose to add music and distinct sounds or text to make a statement which will enable your book to stand out.

Watch other trailers on YouTube to see if there is a similar style you would like to follow. Write down what you like and put together something amazing. Depending on the company, you'll be asked for six to ten or more sentences to tease the viewers. These sentences have to tell a story without telling the story. It's almost like writing a Haiku poem. Sometimes the lines of text will appear on the screen while other times, a narrator will speak the lines throughout the trailer.

The following are texts we used for some of Michael Phillip Cash's books:

Pokergeist:

> Poker was Clutch's life.
> Poker caused his death.
> Telly can't catch a break.
> Worlds and dreams collide.
> Clutch forces Telly to compete for the biggest prize and risk everything.
> In both life and love, the cards are stacked against them.
> They must learn if life is about the cards one is dealt or is it really about how you   play them.

The History Major:

> After a night of heavy partying, college freshman Amanda Greene wakes up to a different world.
> Her roommate is a stranger; her boyfriend has left her; her world has collapsed.
> The atmosphere appears muted and foreign.
> A shadow looms outside her door, making her feel threatened.
> She finds herself in a class she never registered for, with people she can't quite remember.

Will stories from the past help unfold the mystery of these happenings?
Can historical figures shed light on the present to illuminate the future?

Schism: The Battle for Darracia:

A boy on the verge of manhood.
Caught between two different worlds.
Is he strong enough for the Fireblade?
A world with two very different species on the verge of revolution.
Who will win?
Will it be by the might of an army or the strength of a warrior's Fireblade?
Will justice overcome might?

Ren: The Man Behind the Monster by Sarah Noffke

God intended me to die the night I was born.
But an angel saved me.
That was an awful error.
I'm a mistake.
Now I live alone or with the strong and arrogant.
But I don't live close to those who are vulnerable.
I don't live close to those who might dare to love me.
I don't trust myself.
Because I was born with too much power.
I'm Ren Lewis.

Make your book and characters come alive. The trailer can be exciting, suspenseful, mysterious, or teasing. Use the tone of your book to create the tone for the trailer. Use lines from your book description or create a new narrative. Use elements of your book throughout the trailer. Images from your books can be utilized. You painted a picture with words, now create your masterpiece with a video. The music should match the mood.

To Do List:

1 - Consider a book trailer.
2 - Put together six to ten or more lines that describe your book
without giving away too much information.
3 - Create a trailer or find someone to put it together for you.

CHAPTER 11

GET READY FOR BLAST OFF ~ CAROLE WITH A LOT OF SUPPORT FROM JULIE

You have a beautifully-edited manuscript. It's been formatted to perfection. You are ready to rock and roll. Not so fast. You need to get a proof and read it at least twice.

A proof is the first printed copy of your manuscript. It is the template of what your book will look like once it's printed. Any mistakes you find will show up in every copy of the book. If you are not happy with any part of it, now is the time to fix it. Your publisher or POD company will mail you a copy if you request it. Sometimes, you may have to pay for that copy. Some companies will send it free of charge.

If you don't want to spend the money, you can review a digital copy that is a replica of what your book will look like when completed. It's better if you can get your trusty beta reader to do a once over. You would be surprised at the mistakes that slip through the cracks.

To upload your paperback, go to Createspace or one of the other self-publishing companies. Create an account. Make sure you have the file of your book and cover, as well as your bank information (you'll need that for those royalty payments), and you're ready to go. To add a new title for your first book, follow the instructions after logging into your account. Createspace walks you through the entire process.

To upload your Kindle book, go to kdp.amazon.com and sign on to your account. You should have the same information ready. Everything you need to know is at your fingertips. They have made self-publishing easy and fast.

Both sites take you step-by-step and explain the process along the way. You may see little "i" icons as you are uploading your book that you can click to find out more information during some of those steps. They help you make informed decisions throughout the process.

Once you publish your book, you can keep track of your sales and downloads on the author dashboard. You can see your future payouts growing. It is exciting to be able to see how many pages (if you sign up for the Kindle Unlimited/KDP program) are read each day. It's hard not to pull it up and refresh the screen every hour.

When you publish your book, you may notice that each format (Kindle and paperback) will appear on different pages on the Amazon site. Don't worry about that. They will link automatically. Sometimes it can take a few days, but if you notice that it's taking longer, you may want to contact Amazon through Author's Central and ask them to link them.

Each of the publishing sites will also assign your ISBN (International Standard Book Number) and ASIN (Amazon Standard Identification Number for Kindle books) numbers, which you will need to publish at no additional cost.

If you don't want an Amazon appointed number, make sure you buy one. Is this important? There are some interesting arguments on that subject. Some people feel that if these online booksellers go out of business, your books will go with them. There will be no history for your book. I don't think it is an issue, but do the research yourself. Your book is protected once you publish, so there isn't a copyright issue.

To Do List:

1 - Look over your proof, then read it again.
2 - Upload your book title, have your ISBN or ASIN number
   assigned, upload your cover and book file to publishing sites.
3 - Upload your book description, author bio, and photo.
4 - Click your book size which you had already decided on before
   your book was formatted, pick a paper color (cream or black
   and white), and follow all prompts to go through the publishing
   process.

CHAPTER 12

HOLD ON; THERE'S MORE!
~ CAROLE AND JULIE

Are you exhausted? Sorry to say, there's more to do. You have to tie this baby into a neat package. Now is category time.

On Amazon or some selling sites, you will be asked the choose the BISAC categories. These are used by the bookselling industry to help identify and categorize books by their subject matter. They'll be the first category, then subcategories, perhaps including a third. This will make your book come up in searches as well as connect it to groups with similar books.

This is where you select the appropriate genre. Is your book horror or mystery, a thriller, or an adventure? Think about the subcategories and take your time choosing the right ones. This is important; you want your book to come up linked to other books in the same genre. It makes it inviting for the reader to buy.

Amazon and Goodreads will pair your book with similarly themed novels with this catchy phrase,"If you liked this book, then you might enjoy…." You want to reach your target audience as directly as you can. Add key search words, so your book can be categorized. You are allowed five on Createspace. I can't speak for other vendors.

If you are unsure what categories your book falls under, find similar books on Amazon and see what categories they have listed. Do this from a desktop since they won't always show up on a mobile device. The categories will be listed under the "Product Details" section on a book page, right with the ranking. You will also be prompted to identify the suitable audience, whether it's Juvenile, YA (Young Adult), New Adult (NA), or Adult.

Setting The Price

Pricing must be figured out, and it can be a major dilemma. If you price your book high, and it doesn't catch an audience, it may slip into the bowels of Amazon, never to be seen again.

We tend to price our Kindles low. We look to see what other authors are charging for paperbacks and try to keep ours at the same price point. It may take more time to recoup expenses, but we determined that the longer the book stays in, the lower rating for Kindle sales, the more people see it, and hopefully purchase it.

The theory is if you price your book higher, you will make more profit per book, but in the long run, if you price it less and make a smaller profit, you will sell more and make the same or possibly more over time.

Some people price it higher and then offer "sales" throughout the year. This price reduction makes readers believe that when they buy it on sale, they are getting a much larger value if the book has a substantial discount during these sale periods. I don't bother with this. It may work for some, but I would rather have consistent sales instead of depending on price drop days to make my books move with sales or downloads.

You are in a friendly competition against other Kindle or paperback books in your genre, so having the right price will keep you in the game.

Other authors we know feel that when you price it too low, it cheapens what people may think of your book as if they are from a bargain basement. There isn't a right or wrong way to do it. Test the waters. Start a little higher and watch sales. If your book isn't moving, drop the price and see what happens.

Once we realized that we did not hit the lotto with the book sales and were not destined to be millionaires, we decided that the most important goal was to get people reading the book.

Our intention was that if they enjoyed it, they might purchase another one in the series, and we would make multiple sales instead of one. If you don't have a series, but you have more than one book, this can work for you as well. If a reader enjoys your book, sometimes they will buy other titles that you have written.

We also decided early to brand ourselves. Branding means that the author is identified rather than the book. All I have to say is Dr. Seuss, and any reader will know he is a children's author. You are not going to associate him to horror like the famous writer, Stephen King.

Most indie writers are churning out multiple books in a series. It is a smart way to help boost sales. If one book is limping along, it helps defray the losses. It's also a novel way to engage readers. They love following characters and become involved in book clubs and fan sites. Sarah Noffke, the author of four different international best-selling series, runs a popular group on Facebook for authors and fans called "Awesome Reading Marathoners." This group is the perfect place for authors to list their books, plan a schedule, have everyone read your book together, and join for giveaways and other fun. It's like a virtual book club where you get to "meet" the authors you are reading. The group is highly active so you will need to step up your A-game. I recommend joining to watch and learn before taking the plunge and immersing yourself into her world. Take notes and take the time to prepare and plan for your author takeover of her group.

You are now on the road to author nirvana. It's a thrilling moment when you type your name into the Amazon search bar and see your book is ready for purchase. You are in business, poised for the money to start rolling into your pockets. Get that bank account ready for the checks to

arrive. But wait - books don't sell by themselves.
from self-publisher to self-promoter. Get ready, P.T
come.
Similar to bringing a new baby home from the hospit.
prepare for the birth of your book. You need to set up s
media and other accounts to get word of your writings c
will talk more about that soon. For now, concentrate on ɪ ...sning and
everything it takes to get to that step.

Once you are satisfied with the posting of your book, press "Publish My Book" and get ready to rock your world!

There is no need to file for copyright protection because under United States copyright law; your self-published work is protected as soon as you write your book. You can choose to register your copyright for added security, but it isn't necessary.

To Do List:

1 - Choose your categories, subcategories, and keywords.
2 - Determine your audience.
3 - Set your price.
4 - Publish your book.
5 - Get ready to transition from publisher to marketer.
6 - Consider joining author groups on Facebook and see how other authors promote their books. You can learn a lot from those pages.

CHAPTER 13

Do You Kindle? ~ Carole and Julie

We joined KDP, although it does limit your book in some ways. We are not available as an E-book or Nook thus cutting our market. We have found the KDP program has so many pluses that it was hard to resist.

Kindle Unlimited is a program through Amazon that allows Amazon Prime readers who subscribe to the book borrowing program to borrow books from authors that participate in the program. As they read your pages, you get a percentage of the funds from the program. It is split among all participating authors, and your cut will depend on the total pages read when they complete the distribution of funds. It is a good way to make extra money through Kindle sales.

Five times every ninety days, you can post your book free. You can have five free days in a row or split them up. You won't get any royalties for the tens, hundreds, or thousands of books you give away, but you will get a jump in the rankings and maybe a boost in the number of reviews your book receives. Some authors have said it is better to have the free days throughout the week, while others prefer to use free days over the weekend. I would recommend not posting free days over busy holidays. You want to make sure people are around to see your book. Free days are an inexpensive way to get noticed. We observed that if we ran this special on one book, other books by the same author were purchased. This is also a perfect time to invite people to download your book for a review. Many authors send out an email blast alerting reviewers that the book will be free on Kindle during this period.

When you enter the paid ranking system after the free days are over, you should see a little jump in your numbers. We watch our rating daily. If you manage to get into the top one hundred of your genre, sales in Kindle increase. People begin to notice you. You have a good chance to get linked to a lively and popular book. This means that if people are looking at a best-selling, popular book, your book may be suggested as something they may enjoy. This will bring you priceless notoriety. If the rating starts to drop, you can fall into the black hole of Amazon, never to be noticed again.

We start to panic when a book starts to hover in the five hundreds in the Amazon rankings and usually run a book for free for a few days. You want your book to remain in the lowest ranking possible, which means it is selling well. Not only does the book bounce back, but the related books of a series also find new life as well.

Another benefit is the giveaway on Amazon located at the bottom of your book page. You can set up a contest under the heading "Set up an Amazon Giveaway." You select from one of three categories of how many books you want to give away and the order in which to do it.

Random means Amazon arbitrarily picks the winner or winners. Section two is up to the author to choose a lucky number. For instance, you can select a winner every third click. Lastly, there is first come, first served choice. The farther apart you plan to give away your book, the more clicks are enabled. So if you plan that one in every ten entries can win, it will stretch your contest longer and builds attention to your book.

Once you have selected the amount of books and the schedule of your contest, you must blast on social media. Use YouTube, Twitter, Facebook, and Instagram. You can attach your video to entice viewers.

Prepare a template: one for the winners and one for the losers, thanking them for participating and encouraging them to look at your other titles.

Here are a few samples:

"Better luck next time. The end for some, but for others, it's the beginning…." Reference for closing line to *Witches Protection Program.*

"Thank you for participating in my book giveaway contest! Arrrgh! Good luck, Mateys!" Reference to *Captain No Beard series.*

"Arrrgh! Better luck next time. Thank you for entering the contest! See you on the open seas. Being a captain is hard work! Arrrgh." Reference for *Captain No Beard series.*

"Congratulations! You won. Excellent, I'm impressed!" Good for any book.

Amazon makes the process easy. While you are paying for your books, you might get reviews as well as get a new fan! Click the button and make some noise on Twitter and to find new customers to build your fan base.

To Do List:

1 - Consider joining KDP and using their promotions.

CHAPTER 14

AMAZON AND GOODREADS
AUTHORS' PAGES ~ JULIE

Be sure to set up your author page on Amazon. To do this, go to authorcentral.amazon.com and follow the prompts. After you sign into your account and agree to the site's terms, you can type the name of your book into the search bar and connect your published book. Add a flattering photo and an interesting (please) biography; you are all set. As you release more books, be sure to link them to your bio page. If you have a blog, you can add your blog feed so your author page will show any updates you post there.

To create your Goodreads' author page, sign into your account or create one if you are new to the site. After your book is published, search for yourself in the search bar. Click your name, and once you are taken to the new page, click "Is This You?" to request to join the author program. It is quick and painless.

You can also link your blog or website to your author page on Goodreads. Take advantage of this. It will keep your page updated and save you a little time.

When adding your information to your author page, make sure you list a few quotes from your best reviews or any awards in the appropriate spot on the book page. Update this section when you receive glowing reviews. People read this information and will buy your book if they see sterling comments.

1 -   ρ Amazon author page.
2 - Set up Goodreads author page.
3 - Link up your blog or website (if you have them) to your pages. We will discuss blogs and websites later on in this book.

CHAPTER 15

Give Your Book A Voice
~ Julie and Carole

Carole's Experience

My brother wanted to read books but is legally blind. We decided to make an audible book for him, so he could listen to the book instead of it being read to him. My son looked up Audible.com, and we began the process of reviewing actors to read for us. We hired an actor to read my son's first book, *Brood X*. We liked the actor's commanding style. He had the right voice. Don't ask me how we knew, we just did.

We agreed upon a price and time frame. Neither were met. He asked for more money halfway through the job. We didn't sign an agreement; we were rookies then. We did like the finished product but had come out bruised from the process.

For my son's next novel, *Stillwell*, we tested other actors. There was no question that my son wanted a male to read his books, so he chose Dan McGowan. We loved his soothing voice. He took on the characters' personalities, and while he is known for being a stand-up comic, his reading brought tears to my eyes.

We've gone back to McGowan time and time again. He is easy to work with, readily available, and willing to fix things when we realized there were mistakes in the text.

Hearing your book read reveals errors like repetitive words that our editors missed. Often we had to go back to make adjustments to the manuscript. Sometimes, McGowan's interpretation and inflection were incorrect. You must listen to your audio version before you publish it; it's a tedious job.

I recommend reading your book as the actor is speaking it out loud, noting the spot on the recording by the chapter and minutes into the story, then alert the narrator where they have to fix it.

You will be astounded how much there are in sales of the audio version. It is profitable, and people love it.

Julie Did Her Homework

Many self-published authors upload their Kindle book and never get around to publishing a paperback. There is a higher cost if you are paying someone for formatting both Kindle and paperback, as well as the additional cost for the paperback cover. I feel it's a mistake to skip publishing your paperback, but what's a bigger mistake is failing to tap into the audiobook industry. This part of the business is growing rapidly, and it's closing in on two billion dollars annually!

The bonus of creating an audiobook is the fact that you get added visibility because there are fewer authors in the playing field. Less competition means that your book will be easier to find.

Amazon has millions of books available on Kindle. Are they not all audible? There are over one hundred and eighty thousand audible titles. Significantly less competition means it's easier for you to gain some much-deserved attention. Your genre may only have twenty thousand titles to compete with compared to Amazon, where you could be up against more than a hundred thousand competitors in Kindle and paperback versions.

There are a few services that can make this an affordable option if you don't want to pay a flat upfront fee, which can run on average,

depending on the length of your book, a couple hundred to about si..
hundred dollars per title. Get a quote before you start. The "voice" of
your book usually charges by the hour.

Voices.com and ACX (Amazon Creative Exchange) are both companies
you can use to produce your audiobook.

If you want to save money, you can find someone willing to take a
percentage of royalties from your audiobook sales.

To use ACX, visit their site and click "author" after ensuring that you
hold the rights to produce the audio version of your book. If you are
signing with a publisher, either insist that they produce an audiobook
version of your book or retain the rights to do so yourself. Next, create
your profile and find someone to narrate your book. You can listen to
narrator samples and invite people to audition to read your book, or you
can post your book and wait for people to come to you. If you find that
perfect voice, send them an offer to narrate your book. At this point,
you can make an offer to pay for the narration or select a royalty share.
If they accept, they will give you a sample. If you love it, they will
complete your book, and you will be on your way once you approve the
final version. Voices.com works in almost the same way, making it easy
to create your audiobook.

ACX will distribute your book to Audible, Amazon, and iTunes under
an exclusive contract. You can decide to sign a non-exclusive contract
if you do not participate using the royalty share deal and distribute your
title on other sites, but it will be up to you to get them there.

Royalty payments arrive monthly and through Audible. If someone
joins, and your book is the first book they purchase, you get an extra
fifty dollars through the Bounty Program.

Making an offer can be a little intimidating, especially if this a new for
you. ACX tells you what you need to know to prepare you for this step.
Most narrators are part of a union, so they have requirements that must
be met before working on a project. If you aren't paying them a royalty

from sales of your audiobook, they charge at least two hundred and twenty-five dollars per completed hour.

You can find a non-union voice actor and negotiate a less expensive deal. Fiverr is a great source to find them, but make sure you read reviews and get recommendations.

Consider the length of your book when you are setting the price. The final price will be based on the duration (running time) of your completed audiobook file.

You do not have to use ACX to produce your audiobook even if you use ACX to add your book to Audible, Amazon, or iTunes.

We have hired Dan McGowan at www.danmcgowan.com to produce most of our audiobooks. Sarah Noffke, another author, uses Tim Campbell at www.timcampbell.me. There are hundreds of actors willing to earn some extra money, and you can pick and choose the voice best suited for your project. Narrators usually have different voice samples on their websites. Try to pick one that will match the mood of your book. For instance, since we are two females, we felt it was appropriate to choose a female narrator for this book you are reading.

You can also choose to record the book yourself, but you will need a studio and the right equipment for the best results. This option can be more costly because of the time you will need to spend in the recording studio.

To Do List:

1 - Create an account at ACX.
2 - Listen to voice samples.
3 - Make an offer and sign a contract.
4 - Approve final copy.
5 - Get paid!

CHAPTER 16
Reviewing the Situation ~ Carole

Now that your book is published, you need to get word of it out there. Time for reviews. Amazon wants only voluntary, free, and honest reviews. Beware people who offer to review for a fee. Amazon will weed them out and make them disappear, so don't waste the money.

How do you get reviewers? Where do they dwell, and how come some books have so many reviews and others so few?

The first thing I do is make a press announcement. I use a service called Bostick Communications. Some public relations companies can charge thousands of dollars and will shout out your announcement in Times Square. I googled various companies and found Bostick who did the release for around one hundred and fifty dollars. They will write a press release that will get the ball rolling notifying reviewers who will request a copy of your book. You give them the cover, the ISBN, price, where you can purchase the book, description, and a picture and biography of the author.

With their help, I was able to find the right people to read and review our books. Reliable reviewers with blogs that were willing to do it for the simple exchange of a free paperback or Kindle.

You can also create your own press release. Some templates are easily found online and you can use them when you need to prepare your release. When it's ready, you can distribute your release to free or paid distribution sites, like the ones mentioned at bookpublicityservices.com/list-press-release-distribution-websites.

Choose a date for release along with your email address, and the reviewers' requests will start appearing. I always avoid doing a release on a holiday. I want people to be checking for these things, not sitting on a beach.

If you plan to build this into a career, this is where you start a solid foundation. I have a list of people's mailing and email addresses when they inquired about a specific book. Each time a book's been released, more reviewers request it. We keep adding them to the growing lists.

We have spreadsheets indicating if they requested adult or juvenile, horror, paranormal, or nonfiction. The list has grown to close to seven hundred people. Many want e-books; others only read paperbacks. While the postage is costly, pick and choose who is best suited for a review. Try to find people who post to blogs as well as post reviews on the major book sites, so you get a bigger bang for your investment.

As I am currently running the publicity for over fifty books from three different authors, I make it a point to remember these dedicated reviewers during the holiday season and send a card, letting them know I appreciate the time they take to help us promote our books.

Never Ask Them to Write a Positive Review.

All authors want and need honest reviews. Don't be scared of the lesser stars or a critical review. Reading a book is selective. Discerning readers will shy away from a book with only five-star reviews. They can sniff out Aunt Myra's glowing bullshit like a hound dog.

Companies like Tomoson will allow you to list your books so that bloggers who are interested in your book will apply to review it. You can set requirements that will need to be fulfilled like Amazon reviews, blog posts, Twitter or Facebook posts, or Youtube video reviews. Here is a warning: sending your book out does not guarantee a book review.

If you want to make a mailing list, MailChimp.com
with paid upgrades, and it is simple to use. Use thes
fans on new releases, awards, giveaways, and anyth
author related.

Using Google search, locate blogs that welcome sto..... ....
as much as you need them. All these bloggers require material to keep
their posts fresh; giveaways are especially attractive.

Offer to sponsor a blog post with a giveaway. You can give away
paperbacks or e-books on those blogs to keep people talking about your
books long after the review post is published. While the cost of sending
signed books falls on you, you will make valuable friends throughout the
blogging community. Their kindness and generosity have enabled our
books to become recognizable. I can't thank them enough.

We contribute to legitimate charitable events too. We have participated
in many book drives, donating not only our books but other authors'
books as well for needy libraries, homeless shelters, and nursing homes.

Now you are creating a list of readers who will honestly review and
promote your book on their sites. Don't forget to include that press
release letter with all the information about the book as well as the short
bio.

A nice touch when you are mailing a paperback is to include some
swag. Swag is a small gift, a token to make your book stand out. When
I mailed my son's book, *Stillwell: A Haunting on Long Island,* the book
was about a real estate agent and a haunted house, so I made keychains
with an antique looking key on them. I bought them all on the web at a
wholesale site. Oriental Trading, Ali Baba, and 4Imprint have plenty of
fun and affordable items if you want to make your book stand out in the
piles that reviewers receive daily.

I have sent everything from notepads and flashlights to beach totes,
depending on my budget.

e Flip, I sent out beach towels and suntan lotion, suggesting it was
arvelous beach read.

For my cultural series, I was able to print postcards for children to fill
out, making it a reasonably inexpensive giveaway.

If you can't find it in your budget to offer swag, consider offering Kindle
or paperback book giveaways to bloggers with large followings and
interactions on social media or send a simple note of thanks. Make sure
you look at the blog before you send your book. Don't send a science
fiction book to a romance blog. Know your audience.

Bloggers get overwhelmed with requests to review books. Make sure
when you pitch or ask them to review your book that you use their
correct name. I can't tell you how many bloggers have turned someone
down because a generic email was sent to them asking them to review a
book or product. Take the time to include their name.

Whatever you do, please don't send out a mass email to hundreds of
bloggers. They are on to you, and it is one of their biggest pet peeves.
Chances are, they won't even open your email.

You can also visit their blogs and find out if they have guidelines for
making requests. You can find more information if they have a media
kit on their blog or website. Be sure to give the reviewer enough time
to read your book while they are dealing with other jobs, kids, school,
husbands, or exes. A week may not be sufficient time. Some are booking
reviews for months down the road. Communicate. Find out what you can
expect before sending the book.

You haven't left the parking lot on this trip. What are you waiting for?
You have so much to do.

To Do List:

1 - Find reviewers.
2 - Order swag if it is in your budget.
3 - Create a list of names, email addresses, and mailing addresses, noting what type of genre they read.
4 - Keep a calendar and write down estimated review timeframes and when you shipped books.

CHAPTER 17

If You Write It, They Will Come
~ Carole and Julie

Paid and Unpaid Reviews

I send all our books to two paid review sites: Kirkus and Foreword Reviews. While they are costly, I found them extremely necessary. They run between four and five hundred dollars.

Firstly, they introduce your name to those influential people in the libraries and bookstores who get their newsletters. Secondly, every review I've received from them is usually dead on, whether I agree or not. Whatever they pointed out as a weakness or strength in one of our books showed up time and time again by the online reviewers. Lastly, with Kirkus, you may be lucky enough to be selected to be in their Best of the Year List or earn the Blue Star of Exceptional Merit. This was a significant achievement I received on my first book. *Captain No Beard: An Imaginary Tale of a Pirate's Life* was named to Kirkus Best of 2012.

The award was huge, and I wasn't aware of its importance until my publishing mentor at Createspace congratulated me. *What did I know, I thought everybody got them!* After submitting over fifty books to Kirkus, only two have been awarded this honor.

Foreword Reviews has a seal that you can have imprinted on the cover when you receive a coveted five-star review.

Foreword Reviews and other sites such as Reader Views, Moonbeam, Writer's Digest Self-Published Book Award, Independent Book Publishers Association, International Book Awards, National Book Foundation, Indiereader, National Indie Excellence, and Nabe Pinnacle Award have contests where you enter your book in its genre, and they are judged by a selected group of readers, usually librarians. Most charge a fee for the contest entry.

The range of fees is anywhere from fifty to over a hundred dollars a category. You can sign books up for multiple categories or genres. Some contests are flat out two hundred dollars or more. Do you research and look for well-known awards with active sites.

Some people downplay the awards because of the cost. They say you are paying to win. I don't agree. I know thousands of books are entered, and many of them do not win. When you have a book that is recognized, it is one of the best justifications for doing what we do.

As far as I'm concerned, an award is an award. All of our books are peppered with them, telling me we are not wasting our time. For every book that is acknowledged, hundreds are not.

There are quite a few companies that have contests with no entry free, and you can earn substantial cash prizes. A few are Graywolf Press Nonfiction Prize, Hillerman Prize, Drue Heinz Literature Prize, Young Lions Fiction Award, St. Francis College Literary Prize, and New Voices Award. You can find a comprehensive list and details at thewritelife. com/27-free-writing-contests with links to each contest and a description of the prizes. Enter as many as possible.

You can join the American Library Association and take advantage of the many free awards there. Once you are a member, you can send any of your books as long as they are appropriate to their guidelines. Some of these prestigious awards include Caldecott, Geisel, Newbery, and Sibert to name a few.

ıgazines like *Publishers Weekly* and the *School Library*
ıt will not require money for a review. If you score a starred
ıake sure you shout it from the treetops.

BookLife is a website that is affiliated with the magazine Publishers Weekly. You can read articles about other authors, instructional stories with insights on publishing, news, and other valuable nuggets of information. It was created to show independent authors each aspect of publishing a book. The site is geared towards advising indies on everything from writing and editing, design, marketing, and distribution. They have an extensive directory of companies that offer specific services, so you can easily find what you need. Want an agent? They have a listing for that.

Submit your book to them for a review, with hopes that Publishers Weekly will select it to showcase in the magazine. This is where you really want to see a starred review!

BookWorks is an online community designed to open dialog between writers. The basic, or core membership is free. The site was built to help independent authors learn how to do everything from writing to publishing and promoting their book.

It's a place where seasoned writers, as well as indie publishing experts, congregate to share their expertise. You can ask questions and discuss problems with everything from your book to the publication. Here, you have an opportunity to show your work to an audience that can offer advice, even get a sneak peek at your budding talent. They allow you to post up to a two thousand word except for a peer review. Becoming a paid member gets you discounts with Kirkus and other review sites or even discounted ads.

Take the best parts of any review your book receives, whether it is from a blog, magazine, or newspaper and list a portion of them on the book page on Amazon. Acknowledge the source in bold letters. This gives you authenticity, especially if it's a published author, well-known blog, or popular reviewer.

Everyone likes a gracious author, and if you bring attention to them (or their books or blogs), they will likely review your other books. If they are an author, and you draw attention to their book or publication on your page, they get a free promotion.

It also shows how much you value your reviewers, and sometimes, they will take the extra time to write or review your book because of that.

May your editorial comments always be overflowing, grasshopper!

To Do List:

1 - Decide if you want to purchase reviews from publications.
2 - Consider free reviews from online publications.
3 - Enter writing contests.
4 - Add reviews to your editorial section on your book page on Amazon.
5 - Check out BookWorks, BookLife, and other professional sites and explore their many services.

CHAPTER 18

Free Reviewers Here! ~ Carole

I spent five miserable nights going through Amazon's top reviewers, looking for email addresses and blogs. It was tedious, to say the least, but rewarding. Some of these reviewers have large followings and influence readers.

Once I found a way to contact them, I looked at the products they reviewed to make sure I was asking them to read something that wasn't a waste of time. If they only liked thrillers, don't send a children's book request. If they say they don't take book requests, don't irritate them with yours.

Next, I went to Goodreads and signed up for multiple groups to discuss our books. There are threads where you can post your book and let everyone know you are looking for reviews. Send everyone that responds a copy. You can also respond to other posts asking for reviewers. Offer to read as many as you can and let them know that you also have a book. Maybe you will get lucky and they will also read yours. Swapping books with other authors in exchange for a review is against Amazon's rules, so make sure you do not ask for a book exchange. You can let them know you have a new book. If they ask for it, please send or gift them a copy. They have friends who have friends who have more friends. Do the math; it's a win-win.

Many authors have become personalities on Goodreads. They lead discussions and reading groups. They create fan clubs and, not necessarily, for their books. This gets people interested in them and perhaps motivates them to find out about the person behind the comments. They act as monitors in discussion groups. This broad their knowledge of what's out there, and, I'm sure, improves their writing skills.

Another fantastic way to find book bloggers is to use Google's custom search. To find it, type "custom search book blog" into the search bar on Google. The first item that pops up in the results is Book Blogs Search Engine - Google. Click it. Then type your genre in the search bar. Pick a few blogs each day and send them an email with an introduction and your book information after you determine that your book is a good fit and read their policy on submissions.

Since I love to read, I decided to start reviewing every book I read. I went from zillionth place to under the top five thousand in the Amazon reviewers' ratings relatively quickly. It's important for people to become familiar with you, so the more places they see your name, the better it is for you. Visibility is one of the keys to success.

Reviews are important. Many readers are quick to buy a book with hundreds of good reviews, but they often skim over (possibly better) books with five to fifty reviews. Leaving reviews is a thoughtful way to pay it forward by helping another author out. Some will appreciate it while others may not. Reach out and connect with authors on Facebook too.

I avoid leaving one-star reviews, and I hesitate to leave a two-star review. I will leave a three-star review filled with positive feedback that lets the author know what I enjoyed, and what I didn't like as much. I wish everyone were as kind. Three-star reviews (if enough are "liked") will show up as the most liked critical review of a book, which can be useful for authors. It's upsetting to see an author get stuck with a nasty one-star review as their most critical negative review. That leads me to a new topic.

If you are reading reviews for another author's book, you should "like" the comments you agree with (if you read the book) because this helps the author. Please, don't like comments on your book or report or flag negative comments. You don't want to risk Amazon telling you that you are no longer allowed to review books or anything else (yes, this can and does happen).

Another thing: if you or anyone else receives a book at no cost or a drastic discount in exchange for a review, you are required by federal law to disclose that information. Disclosing is easy, and you may have seen disclosures at the beginning or end of reviews online. Simply add to your review, "I received this book at no cost in exchange for my honest opinion." Now you're covered. Do an internet search on the FTC's (Federal Trade Commission) Endorsement Guides. It will tell you everything you need to know about truth in advertising.

To Do List:

1 - Ask for reviews in review groups.
2 - Review other books when you have the time.
3 - Make sure to use a disclosure if you are given a book free or at a discount to review.

CHAPTER 19

TROLLS - WHERE THERE'S ONE, THERE'S MORE ~ JULIE

Be prepared and don't take it personally when someone attacks your book or you verbally online. They will leave inflammatory reviews to stir you up and get a reaction; then they will pounce. People always say there's no such thing as bad publicity. They lied.

Confronting your online bullies who leave nasty reviews (please note, there is a difference between a legit negative review and a troll's review) can be tempting. Believe me; you *will* know the difference, and responding to a troll is the worst mistake you can make. Internet bullies have friends. Lots of them. They will come in droves, relentless in their vicious attacks, leaving one-star reviews and mean comments. If you complain to Amazon or other sites, the website may consider removing some of them, but don't hold your breath. Flag or report them once. Chances are it won't do you any good.

Lucky for you, those reviews are easy to spot, and they usually are a sharp contrast to your other reviews. Readers look at multiple reviews if they depend on them to make their purchase decision. The intentions of those bad reviews are easy to see. Don't get too upset over them. They could be from anyone: a competing author who doesn't play fair, a fan of another author who has deemed you a threat to their success, or a reviewer who you sent a book but he or she didn't like you for some reason. There are many reasons, and none of them make any sense. Some people get off by trying to create drama by "trolling" the internet, so avoid them at all costs. They can leave a path of destruction in their wake, and that is something that is better left as is.

Stay away, move on, and do not engage, no matter how tempting it may be. The last thing you want is loads of negative reviews to bring your overall star rating down. This can have a massive impact on your sales, and it isn't worth it.

That doesn't mean you can't rant in front of your screen while sipping a glass of bourbon. Another thing, don't go crying to your overprotective family and friends. The advice above applies to them as well. You don't want them coming to your rescue in this case.

Legitimate negative reviews will be fair in their assessment although you may not agree with their opinions. They are usually matter-of-fact and back up their feelings with examples or passages from your book. They may have so much disdain for a character that they couldn't finish your book. It's their honest opinion, and you can't expect everyone to love what you write. Many negative reviews list key components that you missed, tell you what was off, or what they didn't agree with in your book. Legitimate negative reviews will almost always explain why they are knocking those stars off, and you should listen to what they are telling you.

You may not agree, but if enough people say the same thing, understand there must be some truth in it. Negative reviews will make you a better writer if you pay attention and learn from them. Open your mind and get over the hurt. Don't take it personally, although you poured your heart and soul into your book. Use their feedback and grow as a writer, strengthening your craft. When they start telling you something consistently, take notice. They are doing you a favor.

To Do List:

1 - Ignore trolls and move on to something else.
2 - Remember there is no such thing as a bad review – yeah, right.
3 - Use any criticism to grow as a writer.

CHAPTER 20

THE POWER OF SOCIAL MEDIA
~ JULIE AND CAROLE

Some people say it's better to start your social media pages long before you publish. It's completely up to you. You may be so overwhelmed and busy with publishing that you don't have time to concentrate and give your pages the attention they deserve.

Starting early will give you time to grow your pages and bring in more likes and follows before your book's release. You can also list your social media links on your book. If you start your pages after your book comes out, that's okay too. I feel it is best to start things when you are ready, and that varies from person to person. That's the beauty of this self-publishing journey. If you are overwhelmed, like most new authors I know, it's okay to go slow and gain your confidence by taking it one step at a time.

The point is to create your social media pages at some point in your journey and spend time on your pages whenever possible. Don't be obsessed with "likes" and "follows." I know, that can be hard when social media has turned into a popularity game.

Facebook uses fancy algorithms which means that those pages with thousands of followers are having their posts viewed by only a small percentage of those people. Want more people to see your posts? You will need to spend money. That being said, Facebook is a wonderful place for both those willing to spend the extra cash and those who are not.

The beauty of social media is the ability to build relationships with fans. If you show them they are appreciated, they won't wait for your posts to show up and comment on your posts. They will type your name in and find you, stopping by to say hi or mentioning that they loved your book. They will drop in to ask when the new or next book will come out. To me, that is a success in social media.

To Do List:

1 - Think about social media and get ready to start creating your accounts if you haven't already done so.

CHAPTER 21

TWITTER - TWEAK YOUR TWEETS ~ JULIE

What is a tweet? By now, most of you recognize the term. Those that are old school may need a little more assistance. Twitter can be awesome, but it can also be frustrating as you try to get your message across in only one hundred and forty characters. You don't realize how short the message has to be until you try to get your point across with all the appropriate hashtags.

Wait, what? Hashtags? That's what we used to call the pound sign back in the day. I can't remember the last time I heard it referred to as a pound sign, come to think of it. A hashtag is used in front of a keyword (an important word) to make it show up in search results.

For example, if you want to make Kindle a search word, add a # in front of it like this: #Kindle. No spaces. If you are writing a romance, use #romance. New release? Use #newrelease. Again, no spaces. Potential fans looking for a book in a specific genre can search Twitter by typing in keywords.

Don't let them miss your posts! You can use several hashtags on each tweet, and they can be useful when you are trying to reach certain people. Want to sell your haunted house book to people that are looking for haunted houses? Try #hauntedhouses, #Kindle, and #ghosts at the end of your short message or substitute words with hashtags throughout your message. Be sure to include the link to your book.

Try something like this: #HouseFlipping just took a turn for the worse in the latest #book by #MichaelPhillipCash. Include your book link. Easy-peasy.

You can also promote tweets (buy ads) on Twitter to reach more people. Also, watch for direct messages from fans and respond when you receive them. Get to know your fans!

To Do List:

1 - Set up your Twitter account.
2 - Start Tweeting.

CHAPTER 22

FACEBOOK GAIN FACE ~ MOSTLY JULIE AND A LITTLE BIT OF CAROLE

You need to set up a Facebook account. Don't use your personal page where people have to send you friend requests, and you have to approve them. Create an author page on Facebook to welcome your readers and fans to your writing world. They can like your page and choose to follow your posts. Keep it warm but professional. The public doesn't need to see Aunt Myra commenting on your posts about some dinner you missed.

Some authors will create a page for a book or a series. If you plan on writing other books outside of a series, I would suggest going with an author page if you want to simplify things. Fans like to chat, to get to know you. Why tie yourself down to updating numerous book pages when you could spend the extra time writing your next book?

Posting is easy: click the buttons, and it will guide you. To post your book link, pull up your book on Amazon, copy the URL, and paste it into your status box. When your book shows up, you can erase your book link and write something in its place. When you publish, the book will remain with the post, and when people click it, it takes them directly to Amazon. It looks a lot better than posting a book link.

This works with other posts too. Let's say a blog posted a review. You can copy the link over and then erase it, using a few lines from the review in your status box. They can click the link to see the review in its entirety. Don't copy the entire review. That is stealing from the blogger. Bloggers have more value when people click to their site, so please don't take that from them. The post belongs to them, and if you are only using a few lines and linking to their post, you have given them credit and hopefully some traffic (when people click to their site to read the rest of the review) by posting the link to their blog.

Sometimes I will use Canva.com or PicMonkey.com to create a graphic to promote or liven my pages. I don't promote them all, but I do ask fans to share the post with their friends. I may use a line from a review or a quote from the book along with the book name if I'm not including the book cover in the graphic. I try to include the price, and if we are participating in the Kindle Unlimited program, I add that the book is free using the program. Free books will encourage people to look up your book.

Don't be intimidated by these programs. I had zero photoshop experience and was able to create eye-catching graphics that fans loved after my first experience using the programs. Some images cost a dollar or more (the nicer ones do), but a few dollars for something that I can use over and over is a real bargain. Sometimes I start on Canva and then add it to PicMonkey because I like their frames and borders more.

With some of our books, we took photos at the beach and made them the star. We did different poses by having the books stand up with the waves in the background. We took pictures of them laying in the sand with the water coming close, the book laying on a beach towel propped up on a beach chair or against the seagrass or dunes, or with a few shells in the picture; we received hundreds of shares after we mentioned it as a summer beach read. You may get a few strange looks, but it is worth it!

We have also used props in our homes. Some books make a nice afternoon read while you are enjoying a nice pot of tea. Set up a tray and a beautiful tea set next to your book and snap a few photos. Sit the book next to a glass of whiskey and a cigar. Carry your book to the diner and take a picture of it next to your plate. Lay your book next to the swimming pool or on a park bench. These have worked for us. It beats the same book link being repeatedly posted. Those get boring. Challenge your fans to take photos of your books in interesting places too and share them with your fans. For children's books, take more playful photos. Use your imagination.

If you want, you can upload those photos to Canva or PicMonkey and add text, frames, and other elements to make your photo look better.

Facebook has Messenger, a messaging service for your personal page. On your author page, fans can message you directly, and messages show up in a message box. If you respond quickly to messages, your page will share an estimated response time that is posted on your Facebook page. We all want to look good, and that is one of the ways that Facebook makes it possible.

Carole Comes Facebook to Facebook with Julie

I had never interacted with anyone on Facebook; now I participate on eight pages. I had to find someone to help, so I connected with Julie and her company, Away We Go Media. Oddly enough, she was on my mailing list. She wrote me asking if I needed help, and I hit the social media jackpot.

She began with Facebook, Twitter, and the pinners of Pinterest. She set up my author's pages on Amazon and Goodreads. I never knew these things existed. To this day, she keeps them fresh and lively, teasing the public with what's happening in our careers, making it funny, relevant, and real.

As an unspoken rule, we do keep personal information private. There is a little icon below your name on each Facebook post. If you click it, you can change the privacy settings for each post.

I keep any posts on my author pages public. Children's pictures, our homes, politics, and personal and religious beliefs are not present. We acknowledge and honor all holidays and unfortunately, the many tragedies that have been in the news lately.

We both recognize this is a business, and we keep it professional. We also realize in this day and age that you can't be too careful, and there are people who can't identify boundaries.

We have both had stalking incidents, and as a result, we are cautious how we respond and block or disengage when something inappropriate is said. We try and keep unsavory comments off the page by continuously monitoring it. Facebook makes it easy to spot because they notify you of any new likes or comments on your page.

Sometimes it becomes necessary to remove comments or people from your Facebook page, which you can accomplish by clicking the arrow at the end of the individual's comment and pick which option you want to use. You will need to hide the comment first. Once you do, another menu will pop up, allowing you to take a more drastic action against them. You can block or ban the person or delete any post or comment.

I have had my moments; Julie can tell you when I got involved, pressed the wrong buttons, and maxed out my charges with uncontrolled boosts. She patiently taught me how to use Facebook to promote the book to the far reaches of the reading universe, stirring interests of my followers.

Julie also creates parties, contests, and giveaways, all done to get people talking. I can almost chart our numbers in the Amazon rankings with how active she is on social media.

You can spend a fortune publicizing and broadcasting your book across the internet, and there are ways to defray the cost. Look for deals. Comb the internet for popular blogs of people with the same interest in your genre and see if they have book tours. I have a group that runs giveaways, making our reach fantastic.

Please, don't buy followers on Facebook or Twitter to make yourself look good. You need fans who want to like your page, fans that want to interact and get to know you. Would you buy friends in real life? Have the same standards on social media.

Meet people. Interact. That is what Facebook represents. Use it to build relationships with your fans. If they are buying your books, they deserve your thanks, and you can show them by writing a few lines as a response to their comments. Like their comments in return. Don't be afraid to ask them for reviews when they tell you they bought your book or are considering it.

Host an event and use Facebook Live to talk to your fans in real time. It's a fun tool that helps you engage with your fans. Make sure you have an excellent WiFi or 4G connection and connect in ways you never imagined. Let everyone know when you will be available so they can make plans to tune into your "show."

Facebook is full of handy features. At the top right corner of each post, you will find an arrow to click. This gives you a menu where you can hide or delete posts. You can also pin the post to the top of your page if you want it to be the first post seen by visitors.
I only use that when we have a new release. Don't forget to unpin it when you want to return to your regularly scheduled programming!

You can block or ban abusive commenters, schedule posts if you are going on vacation, or delete posts. Answer messages from fans daily and be sure to stay active. Keep them coming back.

Schedule posts when you are going on vacation to keep your page active without having to be glued to your computer while your family is having a wonderful time. You can schedule your posts at the beginning of the week and have them post throughout the week. There's no Writers of America need to spend all-day, every day, in front of your computer. You can respond to fans as needed in front of your desktop or use your phone. It is so easy to take control. Use the handy Pages Manager app when you are on the go.

Join author, book, book promotion, and readers' groups on Facebook. You can also join writing workshops and attend writing conventions in your area. There are too many to name. Type into the search bar a few keywords like Kindle, e-books, author, book promotion, or your genre and request to join as many of these groups as you can after reading the rules to ensure they allow you to promote your book. Look up thewritelife.com/28-fantastic-writers-conferences-authors-bloggers-freelancers to find out if there is a convention or workshop in your area.

You may spend days building an extensive list of groups on Facebook or Goodreads to join. Play with keywords and find more groups when you thought you had found them all. Click a button to request to join. Once you are a member of a group, post a book link (when your book pops up, you can delete the link and write in some text) and a quote from a glowing review. I include the price of the book, and one of the benefits of joining KDP is being able to type, free with Kindle Unlimited.

Post graphics in these groups to change things up and leave the link to your book in the first comment, so your book is easy to find. Don't delete it like you do when you are creating a post. If you remove the link in the comments, your preview will also be deleted.

Some people say that there are ideal times to post. I have found that posting in the evening hours works better than posting bright and early each morning. However, when posting important news directly on my pages, I make sure to add it earlier in the day to get the most visibility.

I break it down and post in about fifteen to twenty groups throughout the day and the next day, I will post to other groups. Who has the time to sit and post all day? Not me. Facebook doesn't smile on it either. Posting multiple "like" posts in different groups (one right after the other) will send you straight to Facebook jail, where they suspend you from posting in groups for a set amount of time. No warning. You go straight to jail. Don't panic. It's temporary, but it will force you to be extra cautious and limit those posts per day.

To Do List:

1 - Set up your book or author page on Facebook.
2 - Start posting.
3 - Have a photo shoot with your book.
4 - Consider attending a convention or workshop for writers.

CHAPTER 23

Party Like a Book Star ~ Julie

Want to stir some excitement on your Facebook page? Schedule an online event. Facebook has a tab for that. You can host a Facebook or Twitter online party on your page to engage a lot of people quickly. Everyone loves a party! People can let you know they will be attending in advance. You could announce the party on your page, once you have built a decent fan base, and encourage everyone to invite their friends. Don't make it too far off. Most of my parties are announced the week I plan to host the party. It works best for us that way. Parties are a good way to grow your following. It takes time, so don't expect a surge of a thousand fans. Parties are meant to be fun, so don't get overwhelmed and make it complicated.

Create graphics announcing the party, and if you are hosting one for a particular reason, promote it. Did you win an award; is this a new book cover reveal; did your book hit a milestone? These are all reasons to celebrate, and when you schedule a party, be sure to prepare. Some parties are more work than you realize.

I usually spend a day planning, making promotional graphics and researching. One of my parties for Michael Phillip Cash was to celebrate a book release for *Witches Protection Program*. I looked up trivia on witches and had a trivia party by posting questions throughout the evening. On a few posts, I attached the word "Giveaway" to draw more attention to the post and make it easier to find when I needed to draw the winners. Mention the details of the prize and post them along with a giveaway end date.

For giveaways, I specify on each post how the winner will be chosen. It may be a random winner will be drawn at a specified time. I count the entries and use random.org to make it official and post the screenshot if requested. All you do is count the entries, enter that number in the box and hit "generate" to get your number. Sometimes, I specify if the comment with the most likes will win or if the winner will be picked another way. Make it fun and get creative. Don't forget to mention if your giveaway is open worldwide or only to the United States. Be sure to disclose that Facebook is not responsible for giveaway prizes. I try to have a few prizes for each event, and they have been everything from a Kindle book or paperback to PayPal cash, gift cards, and other "themed" prizes.

Between the trivia questions, I would share details of the book, and I also posted photos of famous witches and had fans guess the witch. Facebook parties are a lot of fun, and when we host them, we get a lot of interaction from fans. You can change up the theme of your party or your posts to highlight the subject of your book.

I like to make the posts educational and fun, but I also like to use the parties as an opportunity to get feedback from fans. Did they like the cover? Who was their favorite character and why? I posted about every five to ten minutes during the party, which can last as long as you like. My parties usually last one to two hours, but I leave the giveaways open a day or two, so the posts continue to remain active.

I teased fans with quotes from books that I displayed on backgrounds purchased from Canva. I also used PicMonkey when I edited a few of them. Remember those sites if you are on a budget. I will be talking about them more.

Each social media site has rules and regulations concerning giveaways. Look them up. They change without notice, and it is important not to break their rules. You may not get reported, but you don't want to take any chances. Facebook and other sites can suspend your account without warning.

Engage your fans, and they will be the best friends a writer can have, often sharing your book links and leaving reviews. Prizes can vary from gift cards and maybe a little PayPal cash to e-books and signed paperbacks. It doesn't have to be expensive. Specify if your giveaway is open to the United States or worldwide. If you give it away, don't hesitate to fulfill that prize.

If an author invites you to take over their author page or reading group, take advantage of the offer. Renowned author, Sarah Noffke, author of *The Luddites* series, once invited us to take over her online reading group for the day to promote books and get to know fans.

It was added exposure that resulted in quite a few book sales. It will go down in history as one of the most incredible takeover experiences in my career as a social media manager, and the fun lasted for days. I met a friendly group of people, and they made the day enjoyable. The takeover resulted in a boost in sales and followers. Not only that, I was able to sharpen my skills as a social media manager. Did I mention how much I love my job?

To Do List:

1 - Consider having a Facebook or Twitter party.
2 - Start planning your party.

CHAPTER 24

FACEBOOK BOOSTS AND SPONSORED POSTS
~ JULIE

Everyone wants a piece of the pie, don't they? Facebook boosts and sponsored posts can pay off. You can start small with a five dollar boost for one day or longer if you decide you want to experiment with ads. See what kind of interaction you get and see if it changes your book rankings.

Facebook will also enable you to build an audience for each sponsored post or boost. What works the best for me is promoting the "Shop Now" button on Facebook. If you haven't added that feature to your Facebook page, don't forget to do that.

Through Facebook ads, you can choose your audience. Do you want your friends, friends of friends, or completely unknown to you people to see your ads? What kind of interests should they have? You can set it up so that your ads target the right people.

When you post ads, be aware there are people that despise ads and won't appreciate them showing up on their newsfeed. They can hide the ad, but you need to watch for comments that they sometimes leave behind. Stay on top of your notifications when you place an ad so you will know if comments are made. You may also want to consider enabling your profanity filter, so your followers are not offended by responses. You can do that when you go into your settings. If one happens to show up and you don't want everyone seeing it, don't respond, instead, click the hide button and delete or ban the person if you want to keep them off your page.

If you have one book, set the post up to take readers directly to your book page on Amazon or leave your book link in the first comment on the post. If you have multiple books, set up the post to take fans to your author page on Amazon.

You can go into your ads manager on Facebook to set restrictions to control the amount that you spend per day if you get click-happy. Hey, it happens to the best of us. This has been discussed a few times in the previous chapters. I wouldn't keep coming back to it if it didn't work for us. To make it clear, we are not affiliated with any of these social media sites, so we get nothing if you decide to try it out. Our goal is to give you as much information so you can make informed decisions. Knowledge is power!

To Do List:

1 - Consider posting an ad.
2 - Create a graphic to use in your promotions, even if they aren't paid promotions.
3 - Don't forget to add the "Shop Now" button to your site and consider promoting it.

CHAPTER 25

JOIN THE NETWORK ~ CAROLE AND JULIE

You need a reliable network of people that will be both honest and helpful. Many have blogs, some have radio shows, and others run magazines. Whether they are an individual that writes reviews or a website that offers services like book tours or advertisements, you have to find the right places to reach the public to inform them why they should be reading your book.

Try to match your book to the right audience. Follow every lead and find new sites that reflect your genre. Make a chart to see which sites impacted the sale of your books.

Children's Book Review, Al Galasso from NABE, Reader's Views, Long and Short Reviews, StoryTeller's Campfire, Publishers Weekly, Indie Reader, The Old Schoolhouse Review, Monster Ink, Open Book Society, Awesome Gang, Tome Tender, Chris The Story Reading Ape's Blog, Lemon Bee Blog, Bernie Nelson from Lightword Publishing, Midwest Book Review, Enchanted Blog Tours, Bewitched Blog Tours, N.N. Light in Canada, David Savage- What's Good to Do in the UK (don't forget the international market - they read a lot too), Pump Up Your Book, My Addiction is Reading, Vicky and Jen, Fire and Ice Book Promos, Worldwind Tours, Shelf Media Group, and Penny Minding Mom are some of our favorites. There are thousands of them on the web if you do the research. These folks have a diverse reach, and their generosity and support have helped build our various brands.

Some of these sites charge small fees as low as twenty dollars, while others have sophisticated advertising options that can cost over a thousand. Go through them carefully and see which one will benefit your book the most.

Talking on forums in Goodreads with other authors is another viable source. There I heard about Author Buzz run by M.J. Rose. She is a best-selling author who reaches out to librarians and book clubs to promote your book. She has a vast network, and while it can be costly, her outreach is enormous.

Look for book clubs and offer to send a copy to each of the readers for a group reading and discussion group. You can volunteer to set up an appointment for a Skype or Facetime session that will allow for questions and answers.

Net Galley allows you to post a free copy of your book for readers to review and hopefully create spin. Book Bub, Robin Reads, Bargain Booksy, and FreeBOOKSY are similar sites where the literary-minded look for the newest books published. Many of them are librarians or people who purchase for the expanded market like book stores.

Some would question, "Why give it away for free?" Sites like these send daily emails to hundreds of thousands of people with books that have interests in a particular genre. They sign up for the mailing list, and when it arrives in their inbox, readers can click the cover and go straight to Amazon to get the free book or get the book on sale. They love to review and usually have huge followings on Goodreads, Amazon, and Library Thing. Others are people who love to read. To have your book featured on one of these sites will cost you. Some are more expensive than others. Sign up for those sites and watch what happens to other books and then decide for yourself.

If you are writing for children or young adults, it is the time to send out flyers to local schools. Some schools will pay a fee for you to spend the day and read to the kids.

A local toy store created a pajama party for me once, where chil
arrived at the store for an all-day bedtime reading.

I've had booths at fairs as well as our local whaling museum. I've done a
children's party. What can I say? I have no shame.

There are a million events around town, so be pushy and make yourself
noticeable. Everybody loves a local author!

Call your local radio or television stations and send them a copy of
your book. They may invite you for an interview to get the word out.
Take them up on it if they do. Send a copy to all the newspapers in your
community. Maybe they will do a feature article.

Little marketing tip: I carry books with me everywhere, giving them
out in grocery stores, shopping centers, the diner, beauty salons, and
anywhere families are congregating. I ask them to leave a review on
Amazon or Goodreads and never imply it has to be positive. Don't do
that.

See if your local brick and mortar bookstore will allow a signing. Check
for book fairs and holiday festivals. If you throw a million darts, one
should hit a target. You never know what connection you may make that
will push you into indie history.

Either way, you can't rely on publishing and the book selling itself.
Don't believe the fairy tale about the person who put a book on Amazon
and made a gazillion dollars. My son wrote an article about his overnight
success that took almost fifteen years of hard work and sacrifice.

If you are going to spend money, make it worthwhile with the right ad.
Try to put your money into magazines that speak directly to a particular
audience. There are inexpensive children's magazines that will contact
you if they are running a special to stretch your dollars, once you have a
working relationship with their magazine.

Bloggers will feature your book on their sidebar (one of the columns on their blog or a special ad section) for a small fee. These little pops of ads are worth it. Books don't go stale, and you can continue to advertise and talk about a book years after it has been released. A twenty-year-old book can climb to the top of the ratings if enough interest is stirred.

Pay attention to what's going on in the world. If you have written a book about a comet, and there is a lot of news about celestial happenings in the sky, use it to your advantage.

Keep a log, charting sales to see which bloggers and ads are the most successful, then return to those. Some blogs to consider are The Eater Of Books, Twenty Three Pages, The Forest of Words And Pages, and The Book Rat. There are thousands of bloggers out there.

Google "book blog" and add your genre to the search bar to find bloggers that would be possibly interested in reviewing your book. Be sure to ask if the blogger is accepting indie books and make sure they read books in your genre before you contact them. If you are accepted, expect to wait a reasonable amount of time for your review. Maybe months. Read their previous book reviews to get an idea of what you can expect if you submit your book. Patience will be needed.

Join author groups like The Independent Author Network. Don't be afraid to exchange ideas. There are a lot of smart people out there, and in general, authors are a generous group.

There are national groups like the Romance Writers of America, as well as chapters in individual states. There is an organization for every genre. Find the one that supports your type of book and go out and meet people. Don't be afraid to ask questions.

LinkedIn is a network of professionals where you can share information or discover opportunities. If you don't have a profile, you may want to create one and add your professional information. You can connect with other authors, marketing specialists, cover designers, and others that you may want to work with in the future.

Don't be overwhelmed by the workload. Ask for help.
getting degrees in communications who would be delig,
their craft as an intern. Retired people have a vast store o
and may welcome being included in more than babysitting
questions; you may be surprised with their answers.

Schools and libraries or what the trades refer to as mass distribution
are essential. It pays to find a place to put your product in their faces.
TopShelf Magazine has a book and author spotlight section where
independent bookstores and libraries will see your book information and
possibly purchase your book for their institution.

The more familiar with your book they become, the more likely they are
to make a purchase. One of my favorite moments was when someone
mentioned they bought my son's book because of all the chatter on the
Blogosphere! I knew then we were onto something.

When my son's first book, *Brood X: A Firsthand Account of the
Great Cicada Invasion*, came out, I took out radio ads. I was in my
go-big-or-go-home mode back then. I realized that one week of ads, no
matter how much I blitzed the radio, was not enough. The sales barely
moved until we reached the three-week mark. Needless to say, it was a
short-lived experiment. I ultimately had to find less expensive ways to
promote his books.

Stacking Promotions

Bookbub, Robin Reads, Bargain Booksy, and FreeBOOKSY (if your
book is free) are all engaging sites to list your book when they are on
sale or need a push. They each cost a fee to use but have given authors
much success when it comes to ranking at the top of their genre. Book
promotion by stacking works is purchasing multiple book features and
running them on consecutive days. The idea is to get your book featured
every day at one of these sites and others like it that you can find online.
The goal: get your book to the top. While you may not reach the top, you
should see significant climbing in the ranks. With an eye-catching cover
and interesting book description, you are on your way. These are ideal

.1d-alone sites to use throughout the year when you want a boost, but when you use them (and others like them) together, you will go far.

Book Tours

There are numerous bloggers that offer book tours. Again, this will cost you anywhere from twenty to hundreds of dollars, depending on the number of bloggers to the length of the blog tour, but it is less expensive than book stacking promotions.

Many of the bloggers allow you to pick a one week tour or longer, and your book will hop from blogger to blogger daily until the end. Some bloggers or hosts will ask for an excerpt from your book, author interview, or character interview to share during the tour, while others may review your book and share your social media links to encourage followers. Sometimes at the end of the tour (or beginning), there will be a book giveaway. Some authors give away Kindles or other prizes to encourage more giveaway entries. Others stick with books. It is all between the tour host and you. Watch your ratings on Amazon to chart how successful the reach of the blog is. If you see that you're selling books, then wait a while and book another tour.

Book Fairs

Remember the annual school book fair they held at your school? A company would display tables of books for you to purchase at a discounted rate. Well, every few months there are book fairs all over the world, where buyers and agents come to see what is new, published, and trending. They have big events in New York, Chicago, and huge fairs internationally in Frankfurt, Germany, China, and Italy. There are dozens of them from Beijing to London, in almost every major European city.

In the States, the biggest name to pop up is BEA or BookExpo America. It is the largest book trade fair in the country. It is always in a major city and the place where exhibitors showcase their upcoming books, mingle and try to sell subsidiary rights both nationally and internationally.

Buyers come to see exhibitors show what is new and exci
are booths from every major magazine, and everybody wl
comes for these three, four and five-day events.

We usually attend through one of the companies we have been
advertising. Publishers Weekly is a respected and world-renowned oracle
in the business. Companies like Foreword Reviews and Combined
Books Exhibit have a significant international presence and host large
booths and display books in all shapes and sizes from authors and
publishers.

We have "paid for real estate," which means a place on one of the
shelves in these booths. The fees can range anywhere from two hundred
to a couple of thousand dollars, depending on how many books you are
showing and if you take out ads.

For domestic shows, we have paid one hundred and ninety dollars per
each book title. International can run about two hundred and fifteen a
title. There are packages where you can buy multiple shows and get a
discounted rate.

There is also the American Library Association and Exhibition, as well
as the American Library Association Midwinter where your book will
get noticed at libraries all over America.

There are opportunities to place ads in catalogs or, in Foreword Reviews'
case, the current issue of the magazine.

It is also an ideal way to get your books known in the larger markets
outside of the States, like China.

Name recognition is important. The more librarians, literary agents, and
perhaps film and television scouts see your name, the more they may
feel they should be reading your work.

You never know what will happen if you send your book to a fair. Foreign rights do sell, so there is always the possibility of one of these events turning into a life-changing moment.

To Do List:

1 - Network, network, network.
2 - Find blogs to write about you. Offer to do a guest post.
3 - Join local authors' groups.
4 - Learn what events are happening locally and become active in your community.
5 - Contact local newspapers and radio and television stations. Send them a copy of your book.
6 - Join a national group.
7 - Consider stacking book promotions.
8 - Book a tour.
9 - Consider booking space or an ad at one of the many book fairs around the world.

CHAPTER 26
Spinning a Web Page ~ Julie

Having a website is a smart way to list everything in one place. Make sure you list your books so when you click them, you are taken to purchase sites. Your author biography and photo should be easy to find; place your social media links where everyone can find them. Have a contact form for questions, and always list a place for awards and reviews.

Websites don't have to be complicated. Try using Wix Website Editor or GoDaddy.com. I was able to put up a website and have it completed within a day; it was a lot easier than setting up a blog. Blogs are free, and there are plenty of authors that use their blogs instead of a website. I'll add a few examples of both below. Don't forget to set up your mobile view so people can pull up your website from their mobile devices. Keep it fresh and always highlight the best of your books. Some people post reviews, but you should make sure to save room for your awards and any magazine, book, or press mentionable.

A few of our favorite author and book related websites include:

https://authorlauradeluca.blogspot.com
https://caroleproman.blogspot.com
https://lindacadosebooks.blogspot.com
https://readingauthors.blogspot.com
www.awaywegomedia.com
www.caroleproman.com
www.ericjaycash.com

www.forewordreviews.com
www.kirkusreviews.com
www.michaelphillipcash.com
www.michaelphillipcash-officialblog.com
www.publishersweekly.com
www.readerviews.com
www.samuelsbooks.com
www.sarahnoffke.com
www.storytellerscampfire.org
www.thechildrensbookreview.com
www.topshelfmagazine.net

Visit some of them and get a little inspiration for your website. For a website, you will need to buy your domain and hosting. If you buy backgrounds, you will also need to take that into consideration. The Away We Go Media - Author Services website cost under one hundred and eighty dollars and that includes paying for different backgrounds (which were under three dollars each) on each page of the website with hosting for one year through Wix Website Editor.

To Do List:

1 - Create a web page.
2 - Keep it fresh and lively.
3 - Visit blogs and comment on their posts. Be social.

CHAPTER 27

PETER PACKS A PIN FOR PINTEREST ~ JULIE

Pinterest is a do-it-yourselfers' dream! It's like a giant bulletin board for ideas, and you can add anything you want from around the web. But did you know it isn't for recipes and home decorating ideas? Plenty of people pin their published book covers to the popular site, and popular pinners will spread the word by pinning your covers to their Pinterest boards if they are pretty or interesting. Now say that three times fast.

Seriously, though, Pinterest is a popular place to stir up interest in your book covers.
If you have a giveaway, ask people to pin your book covers to one of their Pinterest boards and watch it travel as people repin the covers. Anything to make your book more visible.

To Do List:

1 - Create a Pinterest page.
2 - Look for interesting or controversial pins to get people motivated to look at your page.
3 - Get people to talk about you. In a good way, of course!

CHAPTER 28

INSTAWORLD INSTAGRAM AND THE PLUS OF GOOGLE ~ JULIE

If you like to take pictures, Instagram is a handy app where you can upload and post photos. You can add filters to your photos to enhance them or use #nofilter to show off your true colors. Follow book bloggers and authors and engage with your followers.

Share photos related to your books and give people a glimpse into your world. Include one of you doing a reading or a book signing. If you read at a school, please don't show anyone's face but your own. You are required to have parents sign legal forms if you intend to use the images of children in any of your photos.

We took snapshots of the historical sights associated with several of my son's paranormal romances on Long Island. Take a road trip and find evocative images that you can use to tease your readers. Julie links them with all our social media, awarding people when they can identify which book the pictures represent.

Inspire others by sharing uplifting posts or posts about writing. Have fun! One of the wonderful features is that you can synchronize your posts to appear on your Facebook and Twitter page. This keeps your pages more active without any extra work. Many social media platforms allow sharing of files, and you should take advantage whenever possible.

There are other photo sharing sites where you can post your book covers and other images. Flickr and Imgur are two of them. If you have the time, join and share on as many sites as you can. The visibility will be good for your book.

Google Plus, also known as Google+ is another platform to share information. Some people refrain from calling it a social media network. It is a sharing site, and it seems a bit more personal, like a warm and welcoming, small-town community of like-minded people. You can organize people into groups, or circles, and share information based on what those groups are interested in seeing. If you have a circle of author friends, you may share helpful blogs or other promotions that you have used. If you have a circle of fans, share your book awards, reviews, and new releases.

To Do List:

1 - **Set up your Instagram account.**
2 - **Take pictures but don't share images of others unless you have written consent. Be cautious of sharing too much information online.**
3 - **Sync your Instagram account to your Facebook page.**
4 - **Set up your Google account and start creating circles of friends.**

CHAPTER 29

GET YOUR BLOG ON ~ CAROLE AND JULIE

Julie, my high priestess of social media, set up a blog. I was scared and thought she couldn't keep it filled. Well, that's another thing I obsessed about for nothing. I have a small following and a place to post reviews for other writers.

Wordpress and Blogger are the two leading online platforms for blogging. Long time bloggers will have a list of pros and cons for each. Google them and decide for yourself. Go to Canva or one of the hundreds of other sites to create a banner/header for your blog, and then pick a clever background and template/layout for your blog page. Both blogging platforms walk you through the process. After your blog is published, add your book titles and links to your sidebar or create a header with tabs where you can list your social media and book links. Visit caroleproman.blogspot.com for an example of how you can use tabs under your banner to highlight your links.

Add a visitor counter to let you know when someone visits. You can add a globe like I did which allows you to see where you visitors live. I enjoy posting information about my books but also reviews for other authors.

Visit my son's page at michaelphillipcash-officialblog.com for another example. He publishes book mentions and awards. You don't have to post often, but make sure you keep your fans updated with news.

Add photos (beware of being too personal), videos, and book links to make it stand out. Blogs are not a necessity, and you can get most of the same information out through a newsletter. Decide which one you prefer or you can start both. Some readers will prefer blogs while others prefer to subscribe to newsletters.

To Do List:

1 - Create your blog.
2 - Add content to your blog.
3 - Share your posts on social media.

CHAPTER 30

SNAP WHAT?
YOUTUBE AND TRIGGERS ~ JULIE

One of the latest platforms to consider is Snapchat. This is where you pull the latest James Bond move by sending pictures and videos (or snaps) that self-destruct seconds after they are viewed. It is wildly popular among teens, so if that is your book's targeted audience, you might want to educate yourself on the art of self-destructing snaps and join. Adults use it too, and it is growing in popularity.

It is pretty simple, and there are many online tutorials to walk you through it. Love it or hate it, it is another tool for reaching people, and if it fits your needs, take advantage and learn.

YouTube is a popular video-sharing site, and if you are considering having book trailers made, this site is the best for uploading the videos and sharing them. Bloggers can look up your video and use special HTML code to embed your video in book review posts. They can also share directly to other social media sites.

When you are bored and uninspired, you can surf the videos looking for a laugh. I browse YouTube often because it is filled with informative videos that help you with self-publishing and marketing. There are tutorials for everything.

You can also use the site to share your book. Read a chapter, talk about the description, and show the cover. Add your book links under your video to make it easy to find online. Create a video using your phone and tell readers and fans more about your book or why you wrote it and why they should consider buying or downloading it. Upload the video and share it everywhere.

There was a recent success story on Youtube where an author used hand-written notecards that she held up in front of a camera. The cards highlighted her highs and deeply personal lows in life, and it went viral (meaning a lot of people shared it on Facebook and other social media sites), bringing much attention to her debut novel, which was based on her life story. It was one of the most successful uses of Youtube to bring attention to a book that I have witnessed. While the video was going viral, her book hit near the top in her genre, and it stayed there.

Lately, things have settled down for her, but the results were a lot of fantastic reviews and feedback. She made wonderful use of the platform and months later, I am still thinking about her story. Like many others, I purchased the book because of that video. I wouldn't recommend copying her, but find a way to use the platform that is unique and tells your story.

That brings me to another subject. Triggers. If you write a book containing specific content that could be traumatic to certain readers, please label the content with "Trigger Warning" and tell people why. It is considered common courtesy to advise your readers who may be sensitive to certain subjects, such as abuse and rape before they read your book or a book review. It is also a good warning for those who don't want to read books containing sensitive material.

To Do List:

1 - **Download Snapchat if your book is written for young adults or teens.**
2 - **If you are creating book trailers, create a YouTube channel to post your videos.**
3 - **Be aware of triggers in your book and warn others.**

CHAPTER 31
NEVER SAY NO ~ CAROLE

Give me your blog talk radio spot, your blog, your column; it doesn't matter.

Blog talk radio is the same thing as a blog, only with people listening instead of reading. Sometimes it's interactive, with people phoning in live to ask questions. You can also set up a prerecorded interview.

You get on a show the same way as getting on a blog; you have to be asked. Send out books to blog shows you know that will appeal to your genre.

Look for personalities who will work well with yours and write emails, letters, anything. Send a copy of your paperback to them.

When asked to guest blog, try not to say no. Use common sense. Don't sign up for a blog that is a conflict of interest or one that will alienate your readers or fans. When you are asked to write a guest blog, please make sure you get back to the blogger quickly with your post. Always be respectful of the blogger's time.

Be charming and friendly, like you are having a cup of coffee with an acquaintance whether you are responding on a live radio show, or writing answers to a blogger's question.

Most of the time for a published interview, you will get questions ahead of time if a blogger is interviewing you. Take your time and make the answers interesting, but respond with your answers as soon as possible.

If the blogger or radio host interviewing you gives you a deadline, send your answers in early. You never know if an unforeseen issue is going to prevent you from keeping your word. I've always lived by the rule, if you are not early, you're late.

Interviews can be intimidating. Okay, that's putting it lightly. Some people are nervous, and some are downright terrified. Practice. Pull up sample interview questions on the internet and practice answering them until you gain more confidence.

Slow your breathing, try to speak naturally. Some people talk fast when they are anxious. If you are aware of this, you may want to have someone with you during the interview that can remind you to slow down when you are trying to speed things up. Above all, try to relax. I nearly passed out on my first interview. Take a deep breath and understand people will enjoy honesty and humility. They are going to love you!

The interview won't matter if it has anything to do with your book or not; again, people need to get to know you. You have to stir up interest in *you* for them to want to read your book.

Blog talk radio is an excellent way for them to "see" you. After your interview, post it to Facebook, Twitter, or your blog. Before you know it, people will be looking for you.

Ask your local bookstore to stock your books. Arrange for readings at the neighborhood library. I give our books for giveaways at local church fairs and carnivals.

My hair salon was hosting a "lice" event. They were asked by parents to designate a day for kids returning from a camp where a stylist would check them for lice. I volunteered a bunch of my books. Any child that sits through their inspection was rewarded with a complimentary copy. Perhaps they were used to distract the children while they were being examined! Everybody welcomes freebies, and if it helps their cause, then it's a double benefit.

Brand yourself. Harper Lee and Margaret Mitchell are amazing examples of one-hit wonders. Although Lee published a second book, her reputation and following were built on *To Kill A Mockingbird*. It took her over forty years to release the sequel. Both these authors' books are enduring legacies that became classics.

Create a spreadsheet of all the different resources we've outlined, along with the cost of doing them. Pick and choose where you will get the most for your investment. Make a budget, then try to use it wisely. Sometimes you will have to spend.

If you want to put all your chips in for a full page ad in a newsletter or radio blurb, understand once it is finished, so is your opportunity to be seen. Look for specials and bargains. If you know prices, you'll recognize a deal when you see it. Look at the reach of the magazine, knowing sometimes you will have to splurge. Once you advertise with a magazine or blog, they will often offer you discounts to return for another ad. If they don't, ask about it. It can't hurt.

Try and find the most effective way to get your name and book to as many places as you can. While writing bloggers and reviewers won't cost as much as a fancy advertisement, like a penny thrown into a pond, the widening circles of its impact can go on and on for a while. Sometimes plain old elbow grease is the most valuable resource around. If you are going to take the time to write a book, then invest the time to promote it as well.

Most writers today are pumping out multiple books, usually in a series format, creating fan bases that are hooked on their characters. They follow them and wait for the new releases with charming eagerness. They choose to create a brand so that their name rather than an individual book identifies them to their readers.

You can publish a book on a shoestring, using the least expensive tools out there. Avail yourself of the tricks we mentioned. It is possible to do a careful edit. Watch the YouTube videos to learn to format, and by buying a stock cover, you will save money as well.

I have spent anywhere from under a thousand to several thousand dollars to produce a book. The largest costs are mailing paperbacks out and advertising on Facebook or in magazines. You can defray costs by sending out pdf or Mobi versions of your book and avoid buying books and postage.

Our mailing list had grown so large; postage was running over five dollars for each envelope. That didn't include the people overseas. With over seven hundred people asking for reviewing copies, it was an expensive undertaking. That didn't include the four or five dollars I was paying to buy the books wholesale.

I buy prepaid envelopes for efficiency. They allow up to a certain amount of weight, so I can send multiple books and don't have to go to the post office every time to weigh each envelope. I like to include a bonus book to new reviewers so we can get an extra review. We have mailing labels printed instead of handwriting them to save time.

I might have shelved the whole enterprise earlier on, but as I have said, we are a family team, and we decided to see our mission through. As authors, we have been noticed. The books are selling well, and I have observed my budget for advertising has decreased. It appears we have caught a bit of a wave on social media and the burden of cost has shifted.

None of that would have happened without the investment of time or money. Believe me, while I tried many new things and spent money, the actual work of marketing the books took up an enormous amount of my time. Even with the help of a social media professional, and an assistant, I have spent hours perusing all kinds of leads, following up with letters to interested bloggers, not to mention hundreds of interviews. Some things were wasteful; I learned to put our resources where they would yield the greatest results.

When my older son started his career in writing, we sent out manuscripts to literary agents all over the country. They were mostly returned unopened. Today he has both an agent and an entertainment attorney and appears to be on the verge of exciting things.

My cultural series seems to be catching on and selling well. A producer is interested in another one of my books for a television series. I was picked up by an agent overseas for mass distribution in countries like China.

Will it all pan out? Not sure. None of us has any regrets.

For me, this is all about the legacy. In four years, I have written over forty books that have not only won numerous awards but have stayed in the Amazon top rating consistently.

I have publicized both my sons' books totaling over twenty in a wide variety of genres.
I have learned enough to write a book.

Did I make tons of money? Quit my day job? Nope, not at all. We have made enough to keep the engines of this machine rolling. It's not for everyone, and chances are this is not the gig that will make us rich. Somehow that stopped being an issue along the way.

The late Dick Clark was asked how he felt about growing old. He responded that he wanted to stay relevant. I couldn't agree with him more. Writing has made me feel connected to a world in which I thought I had lost touch. I feel relevant and part of an engaging community that treats me with respect.

I have met and enjoyed a new group of incredible people who seem to root for me with the same intensity and gusto as themselves. I adore them all, truly I do. In this writing community, I feel like I have come home. I am happy.

To Do List:

1 - Send out books to blog talk radio hosts.
2 - If chosen, prepare for your interview.
3 - Brand yourself as an author.

4 - Ask local stores and libraries to consider allowing a reading.

5 - Give out books.

6 - Send your information to local schools if you write for young adults and children.

7 - Have fun!

CHAPTER 32
You Don't Have To Do It Alone ~ Julie

Are you still overwhelmed? Social media managers or virtual assistants are a few of the people who you can hire to assist you. Some people hear those words and think there's no way they can afford to hire help. I've worked with a lot of individuals over the years with various budgets. Reach out. It may be more affordable than you realize.

Most of the people I know who help authors are stay-at-home moms who work from home. They may have been bloggers (that own and update blogs) or maybe they are authors too. You would probably be surprised to know that although many have flat fees for services, some will work out a budget based on your needs or wants that will make sense to you. It frees your time, so you can take care of more important things, like spending time with friends and family or writing your next book.

When I started out, I was blogging on a regular basis. I noticed a real need within the author community. So many felt that they had been taken advantage of and lacked the skills and understanding to market their books. I started with two authors, and my education continued to grow.

I had learned so much as a blogger, but trial and error taught me much more. I began to blog less and manage multiple authors' social media sites and online promotions. Reaching out to other bloggers was easy since I had been a blogger for so long. The experience gave me the confidence to fulfill my dream of writing. Now that my book is out, I can relate more to the authors I assist. The first-hand experience gives me even more knowledge to share with my clients and friends.

I've worked for authors on a shoestring budget, and I have worked larger campaigns for authors. Be open about your expectations. That goes both ways. Anyone you hire should be able to tell you what you can expect based on your budget, but be fair in return. Give them time to build up your social media pages to make a difference. Communicate. Find someone you can trust. Get references, and if you don't feel comfortable, move on to someone else.

There are many others out there waiting for the opportunity to work with you. Consider using a marketing intern if you live close to a college or university. It is one way to cut your expenses and have someone that is learning the latest and greatest in marketing.

To Do List:

1 - Consider outside help.
2 - Don't be afraid to ask.
3 - Give the whole process time.

CHAPTER 33
PAY IT FORWARD ~ JULIE

While it may be easy to look at this guide and become overwhelmed, try to take it one step at a time, even if it's a baby step toward fulfilling that dream. Remember, Rome wasn't built in a day. It takes hours of work, and in the beginning, you will have little to show for it.

Start putting your framework together early, and by the time your book is ready, you will have a solid foundation; you'll be ready to start taking the next steps in promoting your book. A few days after making the decision to co-author my first book, I created my author page on Facebook. I didn't have any book updates for more than a year. To keep my page from sitting idle, I would post something positive or inspirational, or I would share another author's information a few times a week. I made sure to invite my friends to like my page and eventually, I had a nice group of followers. It isn't necessary to have everything set up by release day.

Most of us juggle work, family, and friends, and we're already trying to find a few extra minutes or hours each day. It takes a brave soul to start thinking about throwing a new hobby or career into the mix. It will take time and a lot of hard work to climb the ranks. I've seen numerous authors publish their books and think the work stops there. It saddens me because I've seen some marvelous books die a slow death this way. You can't succeed if you aren't dedicated.

We hope this book serves as a guide to fill you in on what you can expect when you're expecting - which would be an award-winning, best-selling book. Have fun with it. Have fun on your pages. Treat your fans as the friends they are. They will be one of your biggest sources of support on book release day, often cheering you on and sharing the news.

Don't let negative reviews bring you down and always try to improve, whether it's writing your next novel or promoting your latest book. There will be mistakes and possibly a few cringe-worthy moments. Never forget to recognize the things you did accomplish and be proud of them. There are many who talk about putting pen to paper, but they never have the courage to push forward and face their fears.

I am sure some of the best authors to come are out there right now, nervously hovering over their keyboards, trying to decide if it's the right time or finding it in them to follow through and realize their dreams of becoming published.

Remember, it's not a competition, and we are all in this together. Indieworld is a society of some of the most wonderful people you'll have the pleasure of meeting, and the best way to get ahead is by having each other's back. Pay it forward with reviews and share information. Help your neighbor and give back to this gracious community of book lovers. You can learn a lot from each other. Grab that bull by the horns and tackle writing, publishing, and marketing your book. The time is now.

To Do List:

1 - Pay it forward and help a fellow author out.

DIRECTORY

Authors

- Alexander Luke
- C.P. Duhart
- Eric Jay Cash
- Keith Katsikas
- Laura DeLuca
- Linda Cadose
- M.M. Hudson
- Mandie Stevens
- Michael Phillip Cash
- Michael Samuels
- Michele Spry
- Paula Cappa
- Sarah Noffke

Blogs and Websites (Some Of Our Favorite Sites For Reliable Reviews And More)

- Allergy Kid Mom's Book Reviews
- All The Hits And Misses
- A Stable Beginning
- Achaeolibrarian
- A Simple Life, really?!
- Away We Go Media
- Awesome Gang
- BESTSELLERSWORLD.com
- Beth's Book Reviews
- Between The Pages
- Bless Their Hearts Mom
- Book Reader's Heaven

- Book Review Travels
- Books Are My Addiction
- Books To Curl Up With
- Carole P. Roman Blog
- Chat With Vera
- The Children's Book Review
- Connywithay
- Country Girl Bookaholic
- Cover Lover Book Review
- Dad of Divas
- David Savage What's Good To Do in the UK
- Day by Day in Our World
- Dig Good Books Achaeolibrariian
- Embracing Destiny
- Every Bed of Roses
- Fire and Ice Reviews
- Five Minutes for Mom
- For Life After
- Fran Lewis
- GA Bixler
- Golden Grasses
- Greatly Blessed (grtlyblesd.blogspot.com)
- Green Frog Children's Book Reviews
- Have You Heard My Book Review
- Inspired By Savannah
- K&A's Children's Book Reviews
- Lemon Bee Blogspot
- Lextin Academy
- Library of Clean Reads
- Lightword Publishing
- Literary Litter
- Long and Short Reviews
- Loving Mommahood Blog
- Mayor of Bookopolis
- Meryl Wright Books
- Midwest Book Review
- Mother Daughter Duo Reviews

- ookshelf
- eading Addiction
- Light (Canada)
- 's Book Review
- Observations from a Simple Life
- Open Book Society
- Parenting Patch Blog
- Penny Minding Mom Blog
- Pink Ninja Blog
- Pragmatic Mom
- Princess of the Light
- Pump Up Your Books
- Raised To Read
- Reader Views, Book by Book Publicity
- Reader Views Kids
- Reading Authors
- Reviews By Teri
- Royalegacy Reviews and More
- Sassy Peach
- Schoolhouse Review Crew
- Sincerely Stacie
- SoCal City Kids
- The Girl With The Spider Tattoo
- The Loose Screw
- The Zen of Motherhood
- This Mom Loves to Review
- Tometender
- To The Moon And Back Blog
- Tricias-List blog
- Vicky and Jen
- WV Stitcher Blog
- XMas Dolly
- Yah Gotta Read This

Book Tours

- Bewitching Book Tours
- Enchanted Book Promotions
- My Book Tour Virtual Book Tour Services
- Pump Up Your Book
- Reading Addiction Virtual Book Tours
- Worldwind Virtual Book Tours & Author Solutions

Book Trailers

- ANIMOTO.com
- www.fiverr.com (you can find other professional services here too)
- LoewenHerz-Creative http://loewenherz-creative.com

Communities And Social Media

- Bookopolis (a community for children)
- BookWorks
- Facebook
- Goodreads
- Google +
- Instagram
- Pinterest
- Snapchat
- The Independent Author Network
- Twitter
- Youtube

Covers

- Ampersand Book Covers http://www.ampersandbookcovers.com and https://www.etsy.com/shop/AmpersandBookCovers
- Bookfabulous Designs https://twitter.com/bookfabdesigns
- Cover Quill http://www.coverquill.com

Formatting Services And Tutorials

- D.L. Morrese https://dlmorrese.wordpress.com/2012/03/01/my-self-publishing-adventure-episode-nine-formatting-your-book-for-paperback-publication/
- Dr. Sandra Peoples video tutorials: https://www.youtube.com/channel/UCGH9ObR4H5Qw4Dit9J_CE0A
- Ebook Enhancers
- Hugh C. Howey https://www.youtube.com/watch?v=7Pi9Y_ElHpE
- Mybookdesigner.com
- Word - 2 - Kindle

Illustrators and Agencies

- Bonnie Lemaire http://www.bonniella.com
- Kelsea Wierenga https://kelsea.carbonmade.com
- Upwork https://www.upwork.com

Marketing Services

- Author Buzz
- Away We Go Media
- BookLife
- Bostick Communications
- Fiverr

Photo Editing

- BeFunky
- Canva
- Fotor
- PicMonkey
- PIXLR
- Snapseed (App)

Publications

- BookLife
- Foreword Reviews
- IndieReader.com
- Kirkus
- Midwest Book Review
- Publishers Weekly
- School Library Journal
- Story Monsters Ink
- Shelf Unbound
- The Old Schoolhouse
- TopShelf Magazine

Radio

- Authors On The Air Radio
- Blog Talk Radio
- Storyteller's Campfire Blog Radio

Reference Books

- *The Artist's Way* by Julia Cameron
- *The Chicago Manual of Style* by University of Chicago Press Staff
- *The Copyeditor's Handbook* by Amy Einsohn
- *The Elements of Style* by William Strunk Jr. and E.B. White

Voice Artists

- Dan McGowan http://www.danmcgowan.com
- Jennifer Groberg
- Tim Campbell http://www.timcampbell.me

There are many other blogs, tours, publications, and companies that we have worked with over the years. We would like to offer our most sincere apologies for the ones that we did not mention. These people have been supportive and helpful in getting our books the attention they needed.

BIOGRAPHIES:

Carole P. Roman is the award-winning author of forty books. She has found a second, third, and fourth career in writing, marketing, and publicizing her books and those of her author sons, Michael Phillip Cash and Eric Jay Cash. Both *Captain No Beard: An Imaginary Tale of a Pirate's Life* and *Captain No Beard and the Aurora Borealis* have received the Kirkus Star of Exceptional Merit. The first book in the series was named to Kirkus Reviews Best 2012. *Captain No Beard and the Aurora Borealis* has recently been given Kirkus Reviews' Best of 2015. Each book in the series has won numerous awards including the NABE Pinnacle Award, ERIK Award for 2013, Foreword Reviews Five Star and Finalist in the Book of the Year, and Reader's Views Children's Book of the Year 2013. Roman is also the author of the award-winning nonfiction culture series *If You Were Me and Lived in...* that explores customs and culture around the world, as well as her new series involving civilizations throughout time.

She lives on Long Island, New York, with her husband and near her children and grandchildren.

caroleproman.com

Julie A. Gerber is the founder of Away We Go Media, a social media management and consulting firm for authors. She is also a blogger at All The Hits and Misses, Executive Vice President/Business Manager at TopShelf Magazine, Assistant Publisher/Director of Social Media at TopShelf Indie Authors & Books, and co-author of *Tortured Souls: The House On Wellfleet Bluffs.* She can usually be found refereeing her sons or glued to her desktop as she works from home. She lives in Georgia with her husband, two kids, and her little sidekick, a doting Pekingese rescue named Abby.

awaywegomedia.com

Made in the USA
Charleston, SC
24 February 2017